THE ENGLISH TEACHER'S GUIDE TO THE HAMILTON MUSICAL

Other Works by Valerie Estelle Frankel
Henry Potty and the Pet Rock: A Harry Potter Parody
Henry Potty and the Deathly Paper Shortage: A Harry Potter Parody
Buffy and the Heroine's Journey
From Girl to Goddess: The Heroine's Journey in Myth and Legend
Katniss the Cattail: The Unauthorized Guide to Name and Symbols
The Many Faces of Katniss Everdeen: The Heroine of The Hunger Games
Harry Potter, Still Recruiting: A Look at Harry Potter Fandom
Teaching with Harry Potter
An Unexpected Parody: The Spoof of The Hobbit Movie
Teaching with Harry Potter
Myths and Motifs in The Mortal Instruments
Winning the Game of Thrones: The Host of Characters & their Agendas
Winter is Coming: Symbols, Portents, and Hidden Meanings in A Game of Thrones
Bloodsuckers on the Bayou: The Myths, Symbols, and Tales Behind HBO's True Blood
The Girl's Guide to the Heroine's Journey
Choosing to be Insurgent or Allegiant: Symbols, Themes & Analysis of the Divergent Trilogy
Doctor Who and the Hero's Journey: The Doctor and Companions as Chosen Ones
Doctor Who: The What Where and How
Sherlock: Every Canon Reference You May Have Missed in BBC's Series
Symbols in Game of Thrones
How Game of Thrones Will End
Joss Whedon's Names
Pop Culture in the Whedonverse
Women in Game of Thrones: Power, Conformity, and Resistance
History, Homages and the Highlands: An Outlander Guide
The Catch-Up Guide to Doctor Who
Remember All Their Faces: A Deeper Look at Character, Gender and the Prison World of Orange Is The New Black
Everything I Learned in Life I Know from Joss Whedon
Empowered: The Symbolism, Feminism, & Superheroism of Wonder Woman
The Avengers Face their Dark Sides
The Comics of Joss Whedon: Critical Essays
Mythology in Game of Thrones
A Rey of Hope: Feminism & Symbolism in The Force Awakens
Who Tells Your Story: History & Pop Culture in Hamilton

The English Teacher's Guide to the Hamilton Musical

Symbols, Allegory, Metafiction, and Clever Language

Valerie Estelle Frankel

Copyright © 2017 Valerie Estelle Frankel
All rights reserved.
LitCrit Press

ISBN-13: 978-1548568832
ISBN-10: 154856883X

CONTENTS

INTRODUCTION

The musical *Hamilton* is a delight, and fans have noticed the exceptionally clever language. Many know the story of its creation, rooted in literature:

> When the composer, lyricist, and performer Lin-Manuel Miranda went on vacation in Mexico some seven years ago, he took Chernow's tome as a beach read. A couple of chapters in, reading about Hamilton as a "poor boy from the West Indies [who] commanded attention with the force and fervor of his words," Miranda saw—and more important, heard—the bragging, swaggering, word-spinning, quick-tempered men of the American Revolution synchronize with the hip-hop rhythms and run-ins that formed the popular sound track of his teen and early adult years. (Miranda was born in 1980.) Soon he was working on a mixtape that mashed up the founding fathers with beat-boxing bruthas. (Solomon)

As Miranda adds: "The moment that cemented it was reading about how Hamilton's writing an essay gets him off the island [St. Croix]....I was like, 'Oh, he literally wrote his way out of his circumstances. That's it! That's everything'" (Binelli). He saw himself and his immigrant family in this moment and continued picturing them. To Miranda this was "Jay Z, Eminem, Biggie. Lil Wayne writing about Katrina! And so, having had that insight very early while reading Ron Chernow's book, I never pictured the literal Founding Fathers again" (Binelli).

This beloved adaptation reimagines the Founding Fathers as rebel rappers played by actors of color, exploring what in meant to be immigrants in a brand-new nation. This rewrite has already had an effect: Students noted of the recast Founding Fathers, "It just made me really proud, and feel good about being American. Like I belong here" (*Hamilton: The Revolution*, 159).

Meanwhile, critics call the musical "a gateway drug that animates a passion to learn more about its subjects, and not just their foibles and personalities but their ideas" (Smith). Certainly, Hamilton biographies, novels, and historical sites have gained a new appreciation. Fans of the musical are also trying other shows. Why not discover the literary terms of *Hamilton* as well?

Hamilton: An American Musical offers every rhythm and rhyme scheme in the English textbook, and so many more examples, with clever sound patterns and phrase repeats. Following these, students and fans can discover anaphora and assonance, all while diving deeper into what makes this musical so special. Why not use it to learn the difference between allusion and allegory, or discover the argumentation strategies many need for Government class? It's perfect for the high school English AP or college English 1 level, with tougher terms for the real pros. With lots of deeper meanings and analysis for fans, there's something for everyone. Let's begin.

RHETORICAL DEVICES

Here are many "poetry terms" students at a high school English AP or college English 1B level will learn.

★ **Accumulation:** from the Latin word for "pile up." This is a list of words or examples with similar meanings in order to emphasize. Hamilton says in "Helpless": "Eliza, I don't have a dollar to my name/An acre of land, a troop to command, a dollop of fame…"

★ **Alliteration** (initial): The repetition of consonant or vowel sounds to start words. In Washington's first verse in "Right Hand Man" he calls himself "The venerated Virginian veteran."

★ **Alliteration** (internal): In "Washington on Your Side" d's, soft i's and s's appear within words, not just at their start: "**I**f Wash**i**ngton **i**sn't gon' **li**sten to **di**sc**i**pline**d** d**i**ssi**d**ents th**is is** the **di**fference: Th**is** k**id is** out!'"

★ **Alliteration** (symmetrical): That is, alliteration containing parallelism, with the two innermost matching, then next two moving outward. Washington cries in "Right Hand Man," "facing **mad scrutiny**/I **scream** in the face of this **mass mutiny**." Mad scrutiny/scream…mutiny reverses the sound pattern order.

★ **Ambiguity:** Use of language in which multiple meanings are possible. Hamilton's telling Angelica he knows she's never been "satisfied" fits the bill.

★ **Amplification:** An expansion of detail to clarify a point: Washington asks in "Right Hand Man," "Can I be real a second?/For just a millisecond?" The second phrase expands on the first.

★ **Anachronism:** A moment that doesn't fit the time period. In "Guns and Ships," Hamilton says the army is "in need of a shower," something they didn't use then.

★ **Anastrophe/Inversion:** Reordering a sentence for emphasis. Hamilton says in "Yorktown," "If this is the end of me, at least I have a friend with me/Weapon in my hand, a command, and my men with me."

★ **Analogy:** Using a similar example to reason or argue a point. In the first Cabinet Battle, Hamilton says, "You're in worse shape than the national debt is in."

★ **Anaphora/Epanaphora:** Repetition of the same word or phrase at the beginning of successive phrases or clauses to set a structure and add emphasis. King George starts several lines with "You'll" for "You'll be Back." In a counterpoint to this, Washington speaks with lots of first person. Nearly every line in "History Has Its Eyes on You" begins with an "I + verb" statement.

★ **Anecdote:** A brief narrative describing an interesting or amusing event. Burr summarizes that when John Jay quit, Hamilton wrote over fifty essays for the Federalist Papers.

★ **Anticlimax:** Expression whose last part decreases in effect from the prior part. There's something of an anticlimax after the great battle of Yorktown when everyone pauses and appears lost in stillness rather than triumph. Further, Washington answers the great, pounding hopes for an end to slavery with an understated "Not yet."

★ **Antistrophe:** Repetition of a word or phrase at the close of successive clauses to feel more structured: "Hamilton says in "Yorktown": "If this is the end **of me,** at least I have a friend **with me**/Weapon in my hand, a command, and my men **with me.**" This technique emphasizes the repeated words.

★ **Antithesis:** The juxtaposition of sharply contrasting ideas in balanced or parallel words or phrases, to make both sound more different. Washington asks in "Right-Hand Man," "How can I keep **leading** when the people I'm/Leading keep **retreating**?" Leading and retreating are such juxtaposed opposites.

★ **Aphorism:** a concise, classic popular "saying." Jefferson's "Every action has its equal, opposite reaction" qualifies.

★ **Apostrophe:** For ties to epic or myth, a person, thing, or abstract quality is addressed as if present. Dying, Hamilton speaks to "America, you great unfinished symphony..."

★ **Archaism:** Deliberately using old-fashioned elements, including language, to link with the past. There are many, such as "Your obedient servant," in the song of that name. The constant use of "Aaron Burr, sir," appropriate for the time, is archaic now.

★ **Aside:** In theater, someone says something quietly to himself or one character that other characters aren't meant to hear, often criticizing or poking fun. There are several in *Hamilton*, often quiet swear words reacting to a revelation.

★ **Assonance:** The repetition of similar vowel sounds. A type of alliteration. "The Room Where it Happens" explains, "Madison is grappling with the fact that…" with lots of soft "a" sounds.

★ **Asyndeton:** Leaving out conjunctions, which makes things seem quicker. Burr's frequent "a bastard, orphan, son of a whore" lacks an "and."

★ **Atmosphere:** In literature, the mood an author creates in a narrative through descriptive language. Hamilton sets up his affair with Maria as he describes the temperature and his churning emotions as well as their dialogue.

★ **Audience:** Real, imagined, invoked, or ignored, this concept is at the very center of writing and arguing. There are several audiences – the actual theater audience, which characters like Hamilton address on occasion and Burr addresses directly in his introductions. There's also King George watching "The Reynolds Pamphlet" unfold or Angelica staying onstage after "The Schuyler Sisters" to watch the events of "Farmer Refuted" from the upper level. A wider audience appears too as the New Yorkers gathering for the Hamilton/Seabury debate. The Chorus, representing Congress, attend the Cabinet Battles. All these moments emphasize the judgement of history as the protagonists speak publically before real and fictitious audiences.

★ **Beat:** A pause, often letting words sink in. In "Ten Duel Commandments," such a pause makes the rhythm work. "Hang on, how many men died because

Lee was inexperienced and ruinous?"/ [pause] "Okay, so we're doin' this."

★ **Blank verse:** This is written in a regular meter but doesn't rhyme, adding extra order and significance to the text. Basically the entire musical rhymes, but a few lines don't seem to until the rhyme pattern is revealed or contain hidden rhymes: "The best thing he can do for the revolution/Is turn n' go back to plantin' tobacco in Mount Vernon" appears blank verse, but actually conceals a rhyme: "The best thing he can do for the revolution is **turn n'**/Go back to plantin' tobacco in Mount **Vernon.**"

★ **Buzzword:** A word or phrase used to impress, or one that is fashionable. Several cutting-edge words of the time being floated about include "uptown" and "Constitution," both suggesting newness.

★ **Cacophony:** Harsh, clattering sounds, as in the word cacophony, which make the line seem jarring. "Constitution" is a clunky, clattering word. "**God** hel**p** me say no **t**o **th**is" has lots of hard letters, making the speakers stumble in their difficulty.

★ **Cadence:** The natural rise and fall of sound that contributes to a melodic pattern. The alliteration and rhythm help create this in many lines of the show.

★ **Caesura:** A break within a sentence where the two separate parts are set apart. This creates a dramatic pause, for a strong emotional impact. "Burr, Sir" is a small caesura where the comma appears.

★ **Chiasmus:** The order of the terms in the first of parallel clauses is reversed in the second. It takes its name from the X-shaped Greek letter chi. "Are we a **nation** of **states**? What's the **state** of our **nation**?" Hamilton asks in "My Shot." This can also apply to sound patterns.

★ **Chorus:** the repeated verse of a song. King George's "Oceans rise, empires fall" returns in the middle of his songs over and over to provide a break between his new verses and a touchstone for listeners. The Greek chorus, meanwhile, is a small group of "townsfolk" that act as the narrators of the story, reacting to what goes on. In the opening number, Mulligan, Lafayette, Laurens, and Washington thus summarize the story to come.

★ **Circumlocution:** The opposite of getting straight to the point and presenting the case directly. Hamilton, stumbling all over himself at his first meeting with Burr, trying to befriend him and discover how he graduated so quickly but unable to spit out the words, provides an example. He repeats this pattern with many hesitations and compliments when he urges Burr to help write the Federalist Papers.

★ **Cliché:** A common expression, which can reassure or bore the audience depending how it's used. Jefferson tells Hamilton "If the shoe fits, wear it," though Hamilton soon takes apart this phrase while refuting him, twisting the cliché.

★ **Colloquialism:** Slang or countrified language revealing one's humble origins (but with a more literary label). "Poppin' a squat" in "My Shot" is certainly contemporary slang.

★ **Conceit:** An analogy of two strikingly different things, which usually fit badly. In "Washington on Your Side," the line "Try not to crack under the stress," makes sense as a metaphor, but suggests the imagery will be about buildings. The next part, "We're breaking down like fractions," thus comes as a jarring twist.

★ **Connotation:** What is implied by a word. "Satisfied" has sexual meanings, as well as suggesting Hamilton and Angelica's shared ambition. Thus when he suggests she hasn't been "satisfied," he offers all these additional implications.

★ **Consonance:** The repetition of two or more consonants. This doesn't have to be at the beginning of words, so Washington's v's r's and n's all count in "Right Hand Man" with "The venerated Virginian veteran..."

★ **Contrast:** Comparing by pointing out striking differences in order to differentiate: The three Schuyler sisters in New York all react differently, with Peggy the most fearful and Angelica the most assertive.

★ **Convention:** The traditional rules of storytelling. *Hamilton* breaks a few, but even the frame story and the flashback of "Satisfied" are conventions seen in other works of fiction.

★ **Counterpoint Duet:** More a term from musicals, but the language of *Farmer Refuted* is indeed clever as the arguers' words match:

> Hamilton: **He'd** have you all un**ravel** at the sound of **screams** but the **revolution** is coming, the **have-nots** are gonna **win this**, it's **hard** to listen to you with a straight face!

> Seabury: **Heed** not the **rabble** who **scream, revolution!** They **have not** your **interests** at **heart.**

★ **Couplet:** A rhymed pair of two lines. There are many in the show like "Oceans rise, empires fall/ We have seen each other through it all."

★ **Denotation:** The strict, literal, dictionary definition of a word, devoid of any emotion, attitude, or color. "Washington on Your Side" is literally true for Hamilton, with no nuances.

★ **Diacope:** This repeats a word or phrase after an intervening word or phrase. "Dear Theodosia" has the lines "And **you'll blow us all away**.../Someday, someday/Yeah, **you'll blow us all away.**"

★ **Dialect:** Unusual language particular to a certain region or era. While there's eighteenth century dialect, there's also street phrasing, as Hamilton explains, "Ask anybody why we livin' fast" in "My Shot."

★ **Dialogue:** Two or more people speaking to each other in the text. Hamilton and Burr are known for this.

★ **Diction:** One's speech patterns or word choice. Miranda actually blends formal 18th-century speech with 21st-century slang – but it works.

★ **Didactic:** Intended for teaching or to impart a moral lesson. Burr tells the crew as early as "My Shot" that they should stop pouting their opinions so publically. His repeated advice to Hamilton qualifies as well.

★ **Double Entendre:** a "double understanding" (often one is sexually suggestive). Hercules Mulligan's "I heard ya mother said 'Come again?'" has a literal meaning – your mother said "Could you repeat yourself" and a dirty one too. For even more "entendres," a "Mulligan" means to redo something – rather like repeating it.

★ **Double Meaning:** A double entendre but with no implication that it's dirty. Burr's "This should be fun" from "Meet Me Inside" could be read as sarcastic if he fears being punished, or actually eager if he anticipates seeing Hamilton punished. The actor and director might make a different choice each performance.

★ **Ellipsis:** Omission of a word or words, often with three dots taking its place. "Now my life gets better, every letter that you write me," Eliza sings in "Helpless," leaving out "with."

★ **End-stopped lines:** "Laughin' at my sister, cuz she wants to form a harem/I'm just sayin', if you really loved me, you would share him" ("Helpless"). Each line is like a sentence, completing a single thought.

★ **Enjambment:** Continuing one's sentence or thought to the next line rather than stopping at the end of a line. The first number narrates, "And every day while

15

slaves were being slaughtered and carted/Away across the waves…"

★ **Ensemble:** The crowd, especially in a play. "My Shot" starts off as an "I Want" Song, as they're called in musical theater, with Hamilton hoping to find friends and seize opportunity. After this, his friends soon join in, and then all of colonial New York. This spread symbolizes the expanding of Revolutionary fervor, thanks to Hamilton's energy.

★ **Epigraph:** Quote set at the beginning of a literary work or at a division to set the tone or suggest a theme. Jefferson starts his first Cabinet Battle speech by quoting "Life, liberty and the pursuit of happiness."

★ **Epiphany:** A sudden or intuitive insight or perception brought on by a simple experience. Angelica, on meeting Hamilton, has the revelation that she's always wanted someone as clever as she is, followed moments later by the revelation that he isn't the marriage she wants to make. Hamilton has huge revelations – mostly the badly-chosen one that writing the Reynolds Pamphlet will solve his problem, and the vision in his final moments of all he did and didn't accomplish.

★ **Epistrophe/Epiphora:** A figure of speech that repeats the same word or phrase at the end of successive clauses. In "Aaron Burr, Sir," Hamilton excitedly gushes, "You're **an orphan**. Of course! I'm **an orphan**."

★ **Epitaph:** A piece of writing in praise of a deceased person. The entire show functions as an epitaph for Hamilton, especially as the survivors sum him up in a few words in the final song.

★ **Epithet:** A term (positive or negative) used as a descriptive or substitute for a name. Hamilton calls Jefferson "Mr. Age of Enlightenment" in the first

Cabinet Battle. The "Ten-dollar Founding Father" is another.

* **Eponym:** Naming something after its creator. "Sam Adams" is used to mean his beer.
* **Euphemism:** Substituting a more polite term. Hamilton's threatening Jefferson with "I'll show you where my shoe fits" avoids words like which body part he'll put it in.
* **Euphony:** smooth, calming sounds. The cut song "Let it Go," as Washington and Eliza soothe Hamilton, has lots of soft "s" and "l" sounds in the phrasing – "Stay alive" and "let it slide" and "listen to your wife."
* **Extended metaphor:** A long metaphor or set of them repeated through the text. The political situation in the musical is repeatedly compared to a chess game.
* **Feminist rhetoric:** Argument or language that uses or examines feminism and its critique of social structures. Angelica gets some of this in during her introduction when she objects to the phrase "all men are created equal."
* **Figurative:** the opposite of literal – use of metaphor, simile, hyperbole, and other poetic terms to embellish the language. Hamilton says his new son outshines the sun.
* **Free verse:** poetry with no clear rhyme or pattern. The one free verse number is Hamilton's dying speech.
* **Homonyms:** The two words are spelled and pronounced the same but have different meanings. King George says: "And no, don't change the **subject**! Cause you're my favorite **subject**!
* **Homophones:** Words that sound the same but are spelled differently. In "We Know," Hamilton says: "I never spent a **cent** that wasn't mine, you **sent** the dogs after my **scent,** that's fine."

★ **Hook:** A narrative hook at the start of a story compels the audience to keep reading or watching. Ending the prologue by Burr abruptly bursting out that he shot Hamilton intrigues the audience.

★ **Hyperbaton:** Excursion from natural word order in various ways, often to call attention: "Say No to This" hopes Hamilton is "in a prosperous enough position to put wealth/In the pockets of people like me: down on their luck," mostly to make the complex rhymes work.

★ **Hyperbole:** extravagant exaggeration. King George insists in "You'll Be Back," "I will kill your friends and family to remind you of my love!" Even if this is his plan, it's unlikely to win back the Colonists' hearts. A more classic example is Burr's "I'll make a million mistakes" in "Dear Theodosia."

★ **Idiom:** Common expression that often doesn't make sense on the surface. Jefferson's "If the shoe fits, wear it" is a little random, though with a long history.

★ **Imagery:** lively descriptions that form a picture in the head using one of the five senses The opening number provides a striking one with "Our man saw his future drip, dripping down the drain."

★ **Incongruity:** A moment that doesn't fit or elements that don't match up well. Surprisingly, historical phrasing and modern slang mash together and even rhyme quite smoothly through the story, as do other anachronisms, like microphones in the Cabinet Battles.

★ **Intertextuality:** The way that one text influences another. While the play is an allegory for current history and politics, the play *Macbeth*, and various Biblical conflicts, with many small allusions, it's also a retelling of both history and the Chernow biography.

★ **Irony:** The contrast between what is said and meant, or the difference between what is expected/appears to be happening and what is actually true. Hamilton's greatest power – his words – destroying him is ironic.

★ **Irony (dramatic):** The audience or a character knows something one character doesn't. Burr refuses to help write the Federalist Papers defending the Constitution because he's worried it will fail and doesn't want to risk his reputation. Meanwhile, the audience knows something he doesn't – that the Constitution will redefine America and create a justice system lasting centuries. Burr also dismisses the Federalist Papers by saying that "no one will read it." Historically, however, as a special insight into the intentions of the founding fathers, the Federalist Papers are the document most frequently cited by the US Supreme Court.

★ **Irony (situational):** Something unexpected happens. Hamilton insists to Burr, Madison and Jefferson that he did not steal from the government. His defense? That he was actually spending blackmail money after having an affair with Maria Reynolds. This is the last thing they expect and perhaps the worst way to make a good defense. More moments of irony follow as Hamilton keeps goading Burr to take action and stand up for his beliefs. When Burr does, it's to defeat Hamilton's father-in-law and take his Senate seat. Likewise, Philip Hamilton sings that he wants a little brother. Historically, after he dies, he gets one who is named Philip.

★ **Irony (verbal):** Someone says something he/she doesn't mean. Hamilton refuses to visit his father-in-law with Eliza, Angelica, and his children because he insists he has too much work to do in "Take a Break." One song later, he sleeps with Maria and begins a torrid affair with her instead of doing his work.

★ **Isocolon:** Parallel structure in which the parallel elements are similar not only in grammatical structure, but also in length. "Talk Less, Smile More," is an obvious example, and the isocolon makes it seem tighter and cleverer.

★ **Jargon:** Highly technical language used by a specific group, often confounding to outsiders. Jefferson uses financial jargon in "Washington on Your Side," explaining he's "Centralizing national credit/And making American credit competitive."

★ **Juxtaposition:** Contrast or combination of unexpected items. In "Guns and Ships," Hamilton asks, "How does a ragtag volunteer army in need of a shower/Somehow defeat a global superpower?" placing these opposites side by side to emphasize their difference. Larger contrasts appear in songs that alternate between dark and light, or characters' tone versus actions, as King George sings the hammy "You'll Be Back," but after the song ends, one of his soldiers comes onstage and outright murders an innocent.

★ **Leitmotif:** A short, constantly recurring musical phrase associated with a particular person, place, or idea. Angelica and Eliza basically always have their names sung with their particular tunes.

★ **Literal:** Saying what is meant, directly. Burr and Hamilton vow to their children, "I'll make the world safe and sound for you..."

★ **Malapropism:** An incorrect word used accidentally in place of another similar-sounding word, usually to show the character's ignorance. It's not a switched word, but a switched pronunciation with Lafayette's stumbled "anarchy."

★ **Maxim:** A saying drawn from life, concisely showing either what happens or ought to happen in life, such as "In New York, you can be a new man."

★ **Metaphor:** A comparison. Hamilton calls himself "A diamond in the rough" in "My Shot."

* **Metaphor (dead):** A "dead" or conventional metaphor is so overused that it no longer makes a picture in people's heads. It's now just a cliché. In "My Shot," Hamilton says Lafayette's pants "look hot." This no longer suggests temperature to the audience.

* **Metaphor (implied):** A suggested metaphor – more "he floated" than "he is a cloud." Eliza insists she's "drowning" in Hamilton's eyes, suggesting they're pools but not saying so.

* **Metaphor (mixed):** Mixing two metaphors that don't go together – this is generally considered awkward writing. Eliza in "Helpless" blends "Down for the count" a boxing metaphor, with how she's "drowning" in his eyes within a line of each other.

* **Metonymy:** A metaphor that substitutes a related item. Eliza sings in "Helpless," that Hamilton is "asking for [her father's] blessing." This is a replacement for asking permission to *marry* Eliza.

* **Misdirection:** Washington, Hamilton, and Lafayette are so much the focus before Yorktown, that it's a surprise in "Yorktown" when Hercules Mulligan is revealed as a spy on the inside.

* **Mood:** How viewers feel through the show, which shades from light to dark, often with very abrupt switches. Though mood and tone are related and often confused, tone actually refers to the author's attitude he's trying to create in the work, while mood is the emotions provoked in the reader.

* **Onomatopoeia:** A word mimicking the sound of what it describes, such as buzz or hiss. The rebels in the tavern describe the shooting they'll do with "pop chick-a pop" and "Brrah, Brrah."

* **Oxymoron:** A figure of speech that combines two apparently contradictory elements. Historians call Washington a "merciful slave master."

★ **Paradox:** A statement that is contradictory, yet true. Angelica sings in "It's Quiet Uptown," "There are moments that the words don't reach/There is suffering too terrible to name" though she's obliquely naming it.

★ **Parallel structure:** Using the same tense and sentence structure (also known as parallel construction and parallelism) to provide emphasis to a theme or idea. The obvious one is "Talk less, smile more" with its pointed brevity.

★ **Parataxis:** Using short, simple sentences to connect ideas, as opposed to conjunctions and longer thoughts. "Talk less, smile more" works here too.

★ **Parentheses:** An explanatory or qualifying word, clause, or sentence inserted into a passage that is not essential to the literal meaning. There's actually the line from "My Shot" of "He says in parentheses" – a musical or play doesn't usually get so explicit.

★ **Personification:** Comparison giving a nonhuman human characteristics. "History obliterates. In every picture it paints, it paints me in all my mistakes," Burr complains in his final song. In a more ubiquitous one, Hamilton wonders over and over when death will come for him.

★ **Polysyndeton:** adding extra conjunctions, makes things seem slower and more orderly. Lafayette chants, "Guns/And ships/And so the balance shifts."

★ **Pun:** A play on word sounds: "My Shot," as in, my chance, is contrasted with doing shots of alcohol and getting shot in battle during the song. There's also a nod to Hamilton's throwing away his shot and being shot at the end.

★ **Quatrain:** A set of four lines, generally with a rhyming pattern. George sings in "You'll Be Back":

> Oceans rise, empires fall
> We have seen each other through it all.

And when push comes to shove
I will send a fully armed battalion to remind you of my love!

⋆ **Redundancy:** Repeating a concept – sometimes drives home a point, usually unnecessary and to be avoided. In "My Shot," Hamilton calls Lafayette a "hard rock."

⋆ **Repetition:** Repeating words for emphasis or other reasons. King George's "Forever and ever and ever and ever and ever…" certainly qualifies, as he uses the lyric in "You'll Be Back" to emphasize this longevity to a rather ludicrous degree.

⋆ **Reversal:** "…But I'm not afraid. I know who I married." Eliza is reassuring Hamilton that they'll be fine, even without a legacy or a lot of money. The second time, Hamilton says it to Eliza, emphasizing his trust in her even when they have a legacy and money but have lost their son. Through this line, he shows that he understands what really matters.

⋆ **Rhetorical question:** To ask a question of an audience without expecting an answer. This serves to provoke interest and engage the listeners. The chorus asks Hamilton several rhetorical questions in the opening number, asking if America will come to realize what it owes him. This is designed to awaken the audience's attention and lead them to the speaker's point.

⋆ **Sarcasm:** Saying the opposite of what one means with a mocking tone. In cut lyrics from "The Adams Administration," Hamilton mocks Adams with "Aw, such a rough life, better run to your wife."

⋆ **Semantics:** Word meanings and shadings that can alter what's being argued. The Reynolds Pamphlet deals with different meanings of being trustworthy and ethical. However, the public condemn Hamilton, who feels he's done nothing wrong.

* **Setting:** Where and when the story takes place. The exposition establishes this as the characters chant the date, though the rap and modern slang make Hamilton's setting less than perfectly historical.

* **Sibilance:** A special case of alliteration/consonance using *s, sh, z,* or other recognized sibilant sounds. Eliza protests in "Burn": "Your sentences border on senseless."

* **Simile:** a comparison using like or as. In "My Shot," Hamilton calls Lafayette a "hard rock like Lancelot."

* **Soliloquy:** One person gives a speech, usually in a play. In a musical, a song often has the same effect. Angelica's thoughts in "Satisfied" count, as does Burr's impassioned desire to be in "The Room Where it Happens" and Hamilton's desperation in "Hurricane." The clearest spoken example is Hamilton's death scene, as he ponders the effect he's had on the world, sharing his thoughts directly with the audience.

* **Spectacle:** Moments in theater more about the special effects than the story, like the chandelier rising and falling in *The Phantom of the Opera. Hamilton* has special effects, especially the turntable, but they enhance rather than overshadow the story.

* **Stanza:** Like a paragraph but for poetry. About the same as a verse in a song. The musical is obviously full of them.

* **Style:** How the work sounds, like the author's fingerprint. Many literary devices and tools like point of view, symbolism, tone, imagery, voice, diction, syntax, and the method of narration help create this. For instance, Miranda's other musical, *In the Heights,* shares with this one actors of color, rap, hip-hop, and a multi-character story about the immigrant experience. It even takes place in New York and celebrates its culture.

★ **Subtext:** Hidden meanings, extra nuances unspoken in words. In some performances, after Angelica and Laurens walk down the aisle before the bride and groom at the wedding, they share a significant look, referencing Angelica's and Laurens's unspoken feelings for Hamilton.

★ **Suspension of disbelief:** The audience in a work of fiction is expected to do this, and just "go with" the fact that the Founding Fathers rap or are reimagined with actors of color. Common in fiction, especially sci-fi and fantasy.

★ **Synecdoche:** A metaphor using a part to represent the whole. Eliza sings in "Helpless," "There's nothing that your mind can't do." The mind is meant to represent all of Hamilton.

★ **Synesthesia:** Describing something with the wrong sense (as in, five senses) to make the reader feel it on multiple levels. This is a type of metaphor. Madison wants to "Follow the scent of his enterprise" in "Washington on Your Side."

★ **Syntax:** Word order/the way a sentence is constructed. At the Battle of Yorktown, Hamilton raps the unusually-ordered, "This is where it gets me: on my feet/The enemy ahead of me."

★ **Tone:** The emotion written into the show. Like most musicals, *Hamilton* has clear ups and downs. The death of Philip (and Theodosia Sr in a cut song) are filled with actual tears, while Hamilton's acclaim are celebrated with goofy joviality. There are many abrupt tone switches as "The Reynolds Pamphlet" is filled with goofy gloating, followed by Eliza's sorrowful "Burn." This is followed by Philip's upbeat character song "Blow Us All Away," followed by the devastating "Stay Alive (Reprise)."

★ **Transitions:** Adverbs and phrases that bring unity and coherence to a piece of writing. At the Battle of Yorktown, Hamilton raps, "**Then** I remember my

Eliza's expecting me...**Not only that,** my Eliza's expecting."

★ **Tricolon:** Words, phrases, structure, or beginnings or endings in threes. Hamilton says he doesn't have "An acre of land, a troop to command, a dollop of fame" in "Helpless."

★ **Trope:** A common theme or device. Hamilton's having an affair and getting thrown out by his wife is such a traditional plot point.

★ **Understatement:** Simplifying the reaction for subtle or ironic purposes. Challenging Hamilton to a duel in which either of them might be killed, Burr takes the cool, gentlemanly path. In cut lyrics, he requests "an immediate acknowledgement [i.e. a deadly duel] or disavowal."

★ **Utterance:** Statement that could contain meaning about one's own person. Burr's comments when he visits Hamilton for his wedding, then sings "Wait for it" are seeing Hamilton through his own frustrations – why is Hamilton's career skyrocketing while his won is stalling, despite his certainty in his own caution, which Burr is certain should work. Nonetheless, it doesn't.

★ **Voice:** The format through which the narrator tells the story. Burr's voice is irritated and censuring as he criticizes and tries to understand Hamilton's success.

★ **Zeugma:** A figure of speech in which one word applies to two others in different senses of that word. Hamilton says at Yorktown, "...my Eliza's **expecting** me. Not only that, my Eliza's **expecting**!"

RHYME

Words ending in the same sound are placed in a pattern.

★ **End Rhymes:** Rhyming of the final words of lines in a poem. Since it's rather a standard rhyme, most lines of the musical do this, for instance, the King in "What Comes Next" rhymes "Awesome. **Wow**" with "Do you have a clue what happens **now**?"

★ **Eye Rhymes:** Rhyme on words that look the same but which are actually pronounced differently – for example "bough" and "rough." This one doesn't appear in the musical, since it's such a verbal medium that writing it down would be of little help.

★ **Feminine/Multisyllabic Rhyme:** A two-syllable rhyme, generally used for humorous effect. Hamilton never punched the bursar historically, but Miranda couldn't resist rhyming the job with "Burr, sir." There's also Mercer. In "Non-Stop," Hamilton impressively rhymes "amendments" and "independence."

★ **Hidden/Concealed rhymes:** "The best thing he can do for the revolution/Is turn n' go back to plantin' tobacco in Mount Vernon" actually conceals a rhyme when one looks carefully: "The best thing he can do for the revolution is **turn n'**/Go back to plantin' tobacco in **Mount Vernon**."

★ **Identical Rhymes:** Simply rhyming the same word twice. In "Guns and Ships," Lafayette asks, "You wanna fight for your land **back**?" and the ensemble retort, "You gotta get your right hand man **back**!"

★ Internal Rhymes: Rhyming of two words within the same line. In the first Cabinet Battle, Jefferson tells Hamilton, "Our debts are **paid,** I'm **afraid**/Don't tax the South cuz we got it **made** in the **shade**." The verse doesn't just rhyme afraid and shade, but two others as well.

★ **Interwoven Rhymes:** a syllable is used at the end of one rhyme pair before appearing at the beginning of another. "Lock up ya daughters and horses, of course/It's hard to have inter**course** over four sets of **cors**ets."

★ **Masculine Rhyme:** One syllable rhymes like "You've been **freed**/Do you know how hard it is to **lead**?" in "What Comes Next"

★ **Rich Rhymes:** Rhyme using homophones (two different words that sound the same) like "raise" and "raze." In cut lyrics from "The Adams Administration," Hamilton rhymes "new since" and "nuisance." He adds on "no sense" (almost a third rich rhyme) for good measure.

★ **Slant Rhymes** (imperfect, partial, near, oblique, off etc.): Rhyme in which two words share just a vowel sound or just a consonant sound. Slant rhyme fits more with the uncertainties of the modern age than strong rhyme. Use of this can suggest pieces not quite fitting together or awkwardness. The technique can also be used for humor. Here, it adds to the rebellious slang of a story being built piece by piece as the self-made hero breaks out of his restrictions. "Insane, Man" and "Mainland" in the opening number qualifies, or "despondent and correspondence" in "Stay Alive." Both are close but not perfect.

RHYTHM

Making a beat by how the syllables are placed together. (This is how the words are naturally pronounced, strung together in a way that emphasizes this beat.) The following are all traditional types of meter:

★ **Anapestic** (unstress, unstress, stress): "When are **these** colonies…"

★ **Dactylic** (stress, unstress, unstress): "**Took** up a collection just to **send** him to the **main**land."

★ **Iambic** (unstress, stress): This is the most commonly used, thanks to Shakespeare and much other poetry.

King George uses this conventional pattern in "What Comes Next": "What **comes** next? **You've** been **freed**/Do you **know** how **hard** it **is** to **lead**?"

* **Spondaic** (stress stress): A spondee is a poetic foot in which two syllables are consecutively stressed. Washington's strident "**Outgunned!**" "**Outmanned!**" does this. Of course, it functions like a shout. Daveed Diggs (Lafayette) notes, "Washington raps in this very metronomic way because that is similar to how he thinks" (*Hamilton's America*).

* **Trochaic** (stress, unstress): "**main**land" rhymes with "**came**, and" in the opening number. Both phrases stress the first syllable and unstress the second.

EXPERT RHETORICAL TERMS

Admittedly, these are harder than a high school English AP or college English 1B level. Useful for those who want to study the subject in depth or impress others.

* **Acatalectic:** Having complete or full number of syllables in a poetic line. Hamilton sings in "Right Hand Man," "I will fight for this land/But there's only one man," lines of the same length.

* **Acutezza:** Wit or wordplay used in rhetoric. Hamilton plays on the meanings of "Satisfied" while courting Angelica and she hurls them back at him in the cut song "Congratulations."

* **Adjunction:** When a verb is placed at the beginning or the end of a sentence instead of in the middle. Have it all, lose it all" from "What'd I Miss?" qualifies.

* **Agnomination:** Rhetorical use of similar-sounding words for effect. In "We Know," Hamilton says: "I never spent a **cent** that wasn't mine, you **sent** the dogs after my **scent,** that's fine."

* **Anacoluthon:** An abrupt change of syntax (structure) within a sentence or moving to new topic of discussion before finishing current one. In "Wait for it," Burr bursts out, "And if there's a reason/He seems to thrive when so few survive, then Goddamnit—"

* **Anadiplosis:** Repetition of the last word or phrase of one clause at the beginning of the next clause. This adds rhythm and cadence and can indicate a relationship. In "Non-Stop," the two men note: "I finished up my studies and **I practiced law/I practiced law**, Burr worked next door." This shows their parallel lives.

* **Anagnorisis:** A moment in a play when a character makes a critical discovery. Hamilton learns Eliza is pregnant, and later learns Burr has defeated his father-in-law. Both are turning points for the character.

* **Analepsis:** Repetition of a word or phrase for emphasis. Eliza's "Helpless" shows up a lot.

* **Antanaclasis:** The repetition of a word whose meaning changes in the second instance. King George's "And no, don't change the **subject**/Cuz you're my favorite **subject**" in "You'll Be Back" qualifies, with the word meaning "topic" and then "dependent. "

* **Antanagoge:** The contradiction of a negative comment with a positive one. Washington tells Hamilton, "I am not a maiden in need of defending, I am grown" in "Meet Me Inside."

* **Antimeria:** Substitution of one part of speech for another (such as a noun used as a verb). It's in common use, but money that Hamilton's "socked" away in "Say No to This" counts.

* **Antimetabole:** Repetition of words in successive clauses, but in transposed order (similar to chiasmus).

Angelica sings in "Satisfied" of "**dreamlike** candlelight/**Like** a **dream**."

★ **Antiphrasis:** Use of words in a sense opposite to literal or ironic use of a single word: "Your obedient servant" becomes increasingly ironic as the enemies correspond.

★ **Apocope:** The omission of the last letter or syllable of a word. Hamilton's "Fuu--" hilariously fits the bill.

★ **Apokoinu construction:** A blend of two clauses through a word that has two different functions, one in each of the clauses. Hamilton does this in "Say No to This" – he explains, "Then her mouth is on mine, and I don't say…" and the ensemble protests, "No, no!"

★ **Aposiopesis:** An abrupt stop in the middle of a sentence, suggesting the speaker is unwilling or unable to complete a thought. Angelica in "Satisfied" can't explain how her sister is feeling and lets Eliza fill in the lines with "helpless" over and over.

★ **Asterismos:** The use of a seemingly unnecessary word or phrase to introduce what you're about to say, like "Listen" when people are already listening. Rhetorically, in fact, asterismos cleverly draws attention to the upcoming text. Jefferson tells Hamilton "Wait!" while beginning a speech in the third Cabinet Battle (cut from the final version of the show).

★ **Atticism:** Expression characterized by conciseness and elegance. "Talk less, smile more" covers it.

★ **Auxesis:** Exaggeration, often with sequential enhancement: In cut lyrics from "The Adams Administration," Hamilton chants, "You're a nuisance with no sense/You'll die of irrelevance" and works his way up to "Sit down, John, you fat m---"

★ **Barbarism:** Use of a non-standard word, expression or pronunciation. These abound, from Lafayette's struggle with the word "anarchy" to the many bits of slang Hamilton and his friends fling into 18th-century speeches.

★ **Bdelygmia:** A rant of abusive language. In cut lyrics from "The Adams Administration," Hamilton gets in a full diatribe of insults at Adams, though in the final version, he keeps his most scathing line.

★ **Bomphiologia:** Bombastic speech, bragging excessively. Hercules Mulligan's introduction, in which he insists he can seduce anyone or anything counts.

★ **Brachylogia:** Brevity of diction. "Talk less, smile more" says it all.

★ **Catachresis:** The inexact use of a similar word in place of the proper one. Lafayette's stumbled "anarchy" is close.

★ **Commoratio:** Repetition of a point with different wording. Washington tells Hamilton to "Outrun," "outlast," and "Hit 'em quick, get out fast" in "Stay Alive."

★ **Dysphemism:** If a euphemism is a nicer turn of phrase, then a dysphemism is an offensive phrase deliberately used in place of a nicer one. There are many name-calling moments like Adams' "Creole Bastard."

★ **Epanalepsis:** A figure of speech in which the same word or phrase appears both at the beginning and at the end of a clause, or with elements of plot points that bookend a scene or story. For instance, the first and last numbers are ensemble numbers, emphasizing the hero's effect on history. Likewise, Hamilton's work with Washington begins and ends with taking up the pen for his commanding officer, as Washington offers him a quill in both scenes.

★ **Epizeuxis:** The repetition of words, such as in "Say No to This," when the chorus repeats "no," over and over.

★ **Hendiadys:** A conjunctive (using and/but/or) rather than a coordinate phrase: Jefferson in the first Cabinet Battle calls Hamilton's financial plan, "an outrageous demand/And it's too many damn pages for any man to understand."

★ **Heteroglossia:** Use of a variety of voices or styles within one literary work. The musical blends jazz, hip-hop, Beatles-style songs and ballads with the central rap style. There's also 18th century phrases, quotes, and manners ("your obedient servant") mixed with modern slang.

★ **Homologia:** A tedious style or redundancy of style. "Farmer Refuted" has Seabury repeating all his words, reading off the paper, as Hamilton breaks the fourth wall to complain about how annoying this is.

★ **Hypercatalectic:** Having an extra syllable (or a few) on the end of a line of verse. George sings, "And when push comes to shove/I will send a fully armed battalion to remind you of my love!" The last line is unexpectedly long, of course.

★ **Hypocatastasis:** A type of metaphor that labels something as something that it actually isn't ("You chicken!"). King George calls the people "Insane" in "What Comes Next."

★ **Hypophora:** A writer raises a question and then immediately provides an answer to that question. Lafayette asks, "Who's the best?" then immediately answers with "C'est moi!" This gives one's argument a sense of having a dialogue with the audience, and arouses curiosity about the answer.

★ **Litotes:** Stating a positive by negating the negative — a form of understatement. ("I am not unaware of your difficulties.") "It's Quiet Uptown" is filled with negation, as Angelica describes the moment as "unimaginable" and "impossible to name."

★ **Meiosis/Tapinosis:** A dismissive epithet, such as bastard, or a humorously dismissive understatement.

33

Hamilton says of the terrible General Lee simply "He's not the choice I would have gone with," a complete understatement.

★ **Metanoia:** The qualification of a statement to either diminish or strengthen its tone. In the cut third cabinet battle, Jefferson calls the revolution "our little independence escapade," making it sound smaller than it was.

★ **Parechesis:** Sound repetition in several words in close succession. Seen in Burr's description of Lafayette in "Guns and Ships": "He's **con**stantly conf**using, conf**ounding the British henchmen."

★ **Periphrasis:** Use of excessive language and surplus words to convey a simple meaning. This may be to embellish a sentence, for humor, to create a grander effect, or to divert. In "Non-Stop," Burr tells Hamilton he should have a much shorter opening statement and complains about the length of Hamilton's speech at the Constitutional Convention.

★ **Polyptoton:** The repetition of a word or root in different cases or inflections. Hamilton says in "Right-Hand Man," "They're **batter**ing down the **Batter**y."

★ **Sententia:** Punctuation of a point with an aphorism or common expression. Hamilton suggests in "My Shot," "Let's hatch a plot blacker than the kettle callin' the pot..."

★ **Syllepsis:** A word modifying others in appropriate, though often incongruous ways, basically a pun that show's off the speaker's wit. The many uses of shot in the tavern scene, from what their drinking, to Hamilton's shot, to the risks of getting shot work here.

★ **Symploce:** A combination of anaphora and epistrophe – starting the same and ending the same. Many songs do this. King George sings, "**My** sweet, submissive **subject**/**My** loyal, royal **subject**."

★ **Syncope:** The omission of letters from the middle of a word, usually replaced by an apostrophe. To make words fit the rhythm, several characters use "I'm 'a" for "I'm gonna."

★ **Tautogram:** A text in which all words start with the same letter. "Hamilton's section of "Cabinet Battle #2" does this for important words: "**M**eddling in the **m**iddle of a **m**ilitary **m**ess."

★ **Tmesis:** The proper name for splitting a word by inserting another word inside it. This is generally a swear word, as with Jefferson, Madison, and Burr's "Southern mother-- Democratic-Republicans!"

★ *Verbum volitans:* A word that floats in the air, on which everyone is thinking and is just about to be imposed. Angelica doesn't finish her thoughts, each time letting Eliza interject that she is "helpless" in the song "Satisfied."

STRATEGIES FOR ARGUMENT

The Romans knew and taught many clever strategies for speech writing, all of which might sway an audience. Hamilton and his adversaries use many in their debates.

★ **Absurdity:** The exaggeration of a point beyond belief. Hamilton suggests they pull out King Louis' head (which is no longer on his body) and ask him if they should honor the treaty. This pushes his argument that the treaty is void to the level of silliness.

★ **Adynaton:** Rhetorical use of a nearly impossible situation for emphasis. Hamilton emphasizes their desperation – to the point of eating their own horses – when he begs Congress for money.

★ **Anacoenosis:** A speaker asks his or her audience or opponents for their opinion or answer to the point in question. Hamilton and Jefferson both do this in their debates, asking why their own opinions aren't best here.

★ **Anthorism:** Counter-definition; redefinition of opponent's term for rhetorical effect. When Jefferson insists in the Second Cabinet Battle "The people are leading," Washington redefines the concept of leading as "rioting."

★ **Apophasis:** Pretending to deny something as a means of implicitly affirming it. Jefferson tells Madison, "I know you hate 'im, but let's hear what he has to say." For an additional sneaky level of meaning, Jefferson in the show seems to hate Hamilton more.

★ **Aporia:** A speaker poses a question as an expression of doubt. This can be deliberate, to cast doubt on an opponent, or an actual quandary. Jefferson has several for Hamilton, including, "If New York's in debt— Why should Virginia bear it?"

★ **Axioms:** The point where scientific reasoning starts. Principles that are not questioned. "Every action has its equal, opposite reaction" is from Jefferson, pointing out unintended consequences and the many sides of history.

★ **Bathos:** An emotional appeal that inadvertently evokes laughter or ridicule. King George's lament that the Colonists are abandoning him has this effect.

★ **Charisma:** A sort of magnetic charm that allows a speaker's words to become powerful. This charm and energy seems to be what Hamilton's friends see in him that makes them whisk him in front of a crowd in "My Shot."

★ **Claim:** A statement that asserts something to be true. The debates, from "Farmer Refuted" to the Cabinet Battles all have Hamilton and his opponents struggling to prove their claims.

★ **Concession:** Acknowledgment of objections to a proposal. King George sings in "You'll Be Back," "You say our love is draining and you can't go on."

★ **Congery:** Using different and successive concepts that all mean the same thing, purely for emphasis. Eliza says in "Burn": "Your sentences border on senseless/And you are paranoid in every paragraph."

★ **Dehortatio:** Imperative advice about how not to act: "Talk less, smile more," keeps following Burr and Hamilton.

★ **Delivery:** How a speech is given, including tone and gestures. Hamilton criticizes Seabury's terrible delivery, while Hamilton's new friends are stunned and impressed by his own passion.

★ **Demos:** The ordinary citizens. Hamilton decides what's best for them, until they are revolted by the Reynolds Pamphlet and turn on him.

★ **Dialectic:** Using verbal communication between people to discuss topics in order to come to an agreement about them. The rap battles use this, though they are characterized by never coming to agreement. In "The Room Where It Happened," in a mostly silent bargaining scene, Hamilton does manage to compromise with the others.

★ **Diallage:** Establishing a single point with the use of several arguments. In the rap battles, Hamilton and Jefferson each argue using personal insults, loyalty, duty, ethics, and finances to back up a central argument.

★ **Dialogism:** A speaker either imagines what someone else might be thinking or paraphrases someone's earlier words, just for rhetorical effect. In the cut third Cabinet Battle, Hamilton tells Jefferson, "…you have hundreds of slaves/Whose descendants will curse our names when we're safe in our graves."

★ **Distinctio:** An elaboration on a particular word meaning in order to prevent any misunderstanding or ambiguity. Arguably "Helpless" and "Satisfied" spend entire songs clarifying what the words mean.

★ **Enumeration/Eutrepismus:** Making a point more forcibly by listing detailed causes or effects; to enumerate: count off or list one by one. In "Satisfied," Angelica counts off three specific points of why she shouldn't marry Alexander. Of course, the counting that stands out most in the show is the "Ten Duel Commandments."

★ **Ethopoeia:** The act of putting oneself into the character of another to convey that person's feelings and thoughts more vividly. Angelica does this for Eliza, realizing in "Satisfied" that if she steals her sister's love interest: "She would say, "I'm fine"/She'd be lying."

★ **Ethos:** Ethical appeal – appeals to one's sense of morality to gain the audience's confidence. Hamilton tries this to bring down Adams. Sadly, this technique backfires in "The Reynolds Pamphlet" – he insists he behaved ethically in government, but the public is appalled that he cheated on his wife.

★ **Evidence:** Facts used to strengthen a claim. In the Cabinet Battles, both Jefferson and Hamilton present their cases, backed by reasons their plans are good for America.

★ **Exigence:** A rhetorical call to action; a situation that compels someone to speak out. Of course, Hamilton and his new friends urge the New Yorkers to "rise up!" and rebel against the king in "My Shot."

★ **Expeditio:** one lists a number of alternatives, and then eliminates all but one of them. In the cut third Cabinet Battle, Jefferson says: "We cannot cure prejudice or righteous, desperate hate/So back to Africa or do they get a separate state?" He then emphasizes the problems with all available approaches, leaving slavery on the table.

★ **Flattery:** Using excessive praise in an attempt to ingratiate oneself with the audience, and make them more likely to accept your opinion. Burr tries but in a twisted way, ingratiating himself to Washington by telling him, "I admire how you keep firing on the British/From a distance." He's more effective using flattery while campaigning as he shakes hands and attempts to "charm her" when he meets a lady.

★ **Hypothesis:** An educated guess, working out that "if" something happens, "then" a result will come of it. King George guesses that the Colonists will repent their foolishness and return to him in "You'll Be Back." Considering Burr's philosophy that doesn't pay out in "Wait for It," and Hamilton's belief that he can save himself through the Reynolds Pamphlet, many guesses in the story blow up on the guessers, which of course increases drama.

★ **Identification.** Connecting with a larger group through a shared interpretation or understanding of a larger concept. Hamilton identifies with America as a whole and fights for a stronger Federal presence, while Jefferson identifies more with his home state of Virginia than the national concept. Meanwhile, Jefferson identifies more with the French cause and Lafayette specifically in the second cabinet battle – a fun nod to the fact that they share an actor.

★ **Ideology:** A way of understanding one's external surroundings. Hamilton sees his country as one nation and thus in need of a central financial system. He cares less where the Capitol is. Jefferson, meanwhile, is loyal to his home state, Virginia, and resists taking on the debts of other states for his secure one. Both their ideologies dictate their actions.

★ **Induction:** Starting with specific facts and drawing conclusions, which may be right or wrong. Jefferson and Hamilton both use financial facts to support their causes.

★ **Inference:** Arriving at a conclusion using known evidence or premises and logically forming an opinion. Again, a staple of the rap battles.

★ *In loco parentis:* "In place of parents" – acting on behalf of someone as a guardian might do. Hercules Mulligan uses this phrase in "My Shot."

★ **Indignatio:** To arouse indignation in the audience. At Hamilton's threat to show Jefferson "where my shoe fits" the congressmen shriek in shock.

★ **Kairos:** "timing" or "the right circumstances." Burr, Washington, and Hamilton struggle with the right times to make their decisions, waiting versus acting.

★ **Logos:** Making one's case through logic and facts. In "Non-Stop," Hamilton insists the people need the Constitution and he determines to write essays supporting this. However, the logical case he makes doesn't convince Burr.

★ **Occupatio:** Introducing and responding to one's opponents' arguments before they have the opportunity to bring them up. The opposite of apophasis. In the second Cabinet Battle, Jefferson says, "I know that Alexander Hamilton is here and he/Would rather not have this debate," anticipating the other man's objection then shooting it down.

★ **Oictos:** A show of pity or compassion. Jefferson and Madison pointedly sympathize with Hamilton after his tragedy.

★ **Pathos:** Emotional appeal to excite readers and involve them in the argument. Of course, there are many emotional moments for Hamilton, with the strongest centering on his son.

★ **Position/Purpose/Thesis:** What the speaker or writer is trying to prove or argue. Jefferson and Hamilton clearly lay these out, unlike Burr.

★ **Pragmatism:** Approach based on practical consideration, not ethical arguments. Hamilton rejects Jefferson's superiority to retort, "Welcome to the present, we're running a real nation."

★ **Propaganda:** An advertisement presented to help or harm a person or group. Burr campaigns, telling

40

people he's good for the country and Jefferson isn't, though he doesn't commit to specific ideologies.

★ **Public sphere:** Place where individuals can engage in discussion. "Farmer Refuted" does this in the open street.

★ **Quaestiones:** Debatable points around which disputes are centered. Both Cabinet Battles have these.

★ **Rebuttal:** A chance to refute what the other side has said. In both Cabinet Meetings, Jefferson speaks and then Hamilton gets a rebuttal, trying to disprove his statements and claim. Both times, Hamilton succeeds.

★ **Scare-line:** A word or phrase that is used to frighten the reader, or smear an opposing candidate. Seabury insists, "Heed not the rabble who scream, revolution!" trying to make some Colonists back down from their extreme views.

★ **Tautology:** The same idea repeated in different words. Madison says of Burr in "The Election of 1800": "Ask him a question: it glances off, he obfuscates, he dances." This is the same concept three times.

★ **Validity:** Apprehension over the structure of an argument. Hamilton protests that Seabury is reading a prepared speech and won't debate with him.

LOGICAL FALLACIES

★ **Ad hominem:** Attack on the person making the case instead of his issues (a classic logical fallacy). In the first Cabinet Battle, Hamilton mocks Jefferson for owning slaves and also for the war record not remotely applicable to the conversation as a way of discrediting him.

★ **Ambiguity:** Being unclear to muddle the issue. In "Your Obedient Servant," as Burr demands an apology or a challenge, Hamilton retorts with the confusing, "Even if I said what you think I said/You would need to cite a more specific grievance."

★ **Appeal to authority** (*argumentum ad verecundiam*): An assertion is deemed true because of the position or authority of the person asserting it. If the Great General Washington says it, it must be true. In the cut "One Last Ride," Washington ends the rebellion by appearing in person while he and Hamilton insist on a surrender because of Washington's momentous reputation.

★ **Appeal to consequences** (*argumentum ad consequentiam*): The consequences from some course of action are the great problem here. Madison protests in the cut third Cabinet Battle, "Hamilton, if we support emancipation/Every single slave owner will demand compensation." Even if this is the right thing to do, it will cost too much.

★ **Appeal to emotion:** An argument is made due to the manipulation of emotions, rather than the use of valid reasoning. Burr campaigns on flattery and the people's dislike of Hamilton, then Jefferson. He never clearly takes a stand on issues.

★ **Appeal to fear:** An argument is made by increasing fear towards the opposing side. In "One Last Time," Hamilton protests Washington's retirement with "Mr. President, they will say you're weak." Washington, however, rejects this.

★ **Appeal to motive:** A subtype of ad hominem that dismisses an idea by questioning the motives of its proposer. Hamilton attacks Jefferson by insisting he wants slavery to continue so he can have an affair with his slaves in the cut third Cabinet Battle.

★ **Appeal to pity:** An argument attempts to induce pity to sway opponents. Jefferson pushes listeners to support the Revolution because Lafayette is in danger, in the Second Cabinet Battle.

★ **Appeal to popularity** (Band Wagon): Insisting

something is good because it is popular. Jefferson's insistence on slave trade, however evil, comes from the fact that so many Southerners insist on it.

★ **Appeal to ridicule:** One argues by presenting the opponent's argument in a way that makes it appear ludicrous. In the Second Cabinet Battle, Hamilton's insistence that they ask the dead king's head in a basket for advice makes Jefferson seem silly.

★ **Appeal to spite:** An argument is made through exploiting people's bitterness towards the opposition. Burr asserts that he can win a senate seat against Hamilton's father-in-law without a platform because "they don't like *you.*"

★ **Appeal to tradition:** Someone argues that something is correct because it is customary. Hamilton protests Washington's leaving because leaders don't do that, and King George reacts similarly in his own follow-up song.

★ **Argument to moderation** (false compromise, middle ground): Assuming that the compromise between two positions is always correct. Washington is presented as the middle ground in Cabinet Battles. In the third cut battle, he insists on delaying a decision on slavery. This seems like the middle ground, but in fact causes the Civil War.

★ **Argument from repetition** (*argumentum ad nauseam, argumentum ad infinitum*): Emphasizes that it has been discussed extensively until nobody cares to discuss it anymore. In the cut third Cabinet Battle, Washington appears to end the slavery debate for this reason.

★ **Bait and switch:** One thing is offered and then something less desired is given. A cut scene, with Eliza and Philip meeting Burr in town in 'Schuyler Defeated,' compares Philip and Theodosia as accomplished adults of the same age, both excelling in Latin and French (Dreamcatcher). "This scene seems to foreshadow a happy suitability and perhaps a romance despite their fathers' feuding, subversively preparing the audience for a happy end before the extra shock of Philip's tragedy" (Frankel).

★ **Begging the question** (*petitio principii*): Providing what is essentially the conclusion of the argument as a premise. In the cut third Cabinet Battle, Jefferson leaps ahead to say "But for a second, let us say that we can legislate/Unanimous emancipation."

★ **Circular reasoning:** Burr argues many times that because his position is caution he has to take a cautious position on this issue or that issue.

★ **Dogmatism:** The unwillingness to even consider the opponent's argument, even when many, perhaps millions, of other people believe otherwise. King George suffers from this, as (arguably) do Hamilton and Jefferson.

★ **False analogy:** Believing two situations are similar enough to be treated the same way. In the Second Cabinet Battle, Jefferson insists a revolution like their own needs them. However, Washington tells Jefferson that while he championed the American Revolution, he finds the French Revolution bloodthirsty and disorganized.

★ **False consciousness:** A distorted view of reality, people, and the world. Hamilton and Burr each arguably have this, as Burr thinks waiting and holding back will gain him political power, and Hamilton thinks publically admitting to adultery will save him from scandal. They're both self-destructively wrong.

★ **False dilemma** (false dichotomy, either/or fallacy): Two alternative statements are held to be the only options, when in reality there are more. Hamilton worries that he must be a war hero, or he and Eliza will always be poor. Washington stresses that there are more possibilities.

★ **Hasty generalization** (nonrepresentative sample): The idea that because this happens sometimes or to a small group, it happens everywhere. Seabury insists that because people like him and those he knows don't want a revolution, the entire Thirteen Colonies don't. He's wrong.

★ **Homunculus fallacy:** A "middle-man" is used for explanation, which gets the arguer stuck on the concept. Eliza insists that the little voices in Hamilton's head are blocking him from accepting what his life is and being happy as she describes "The worlds you keep erasing and creating in your mind" in "That would Be Enough."

★ **Hypocritical:** Blaming someone for something the speaker does as well. Jefferson insults Hamilton's fashion, insisting he dresses like "fake royalty" – while he himself is the one in the bright purple coat. Burr, flirting with Angelica, tells her accusatively that she smells like her father has money but insists he's reliable since he's rich. She's completely disgusted.

★ **Moral equivalency:** The implication that two moral issues carry the same weight or are essentially similar. Jefferson keeps putting states' rights as equally important to the rights of suffering slaves, to Hamilton's disgust.

★ **Non sequitor:** A fact or argument that "does not follow." "At least I was honest with our money!" Hamilton says, as the country rises against him because of his scandalous affair. While true, this does not answer the charge against him.

★ ***Post hoc ergo propter hoc*** (Latin for "after this, therefore because of this). Also called False Cause, implying one thing has caused another without proof: In the cut "One Last Ride," Hamilton insists to Washington, "Because it is your Secretary of State, Thomas Jefferson/Who has been agitating these men to rebellion." Jefferson's speeches have not caused the Whiskey rebellion, though one happened then the other.

★ **Red herring:** A speaker attempts to distract an audience by introducing an off-topic point, which draws attention away from the subject of argument. In a cut line from "The Adams Administration," Hamilton (unfairly) distracts from the topic at hand with "Give my regards to Abigail/Next time you write about my lack of moral compass." Obviously, whatever Abigail has done is off topic to a Hamilton–Adams argument.

★ **Slippery slope:** Someone claims that one action will result in a chain reaction of events (the "slippery slope") leading up to a harmful consequence. In the Second Cabinet Battle, Hamilton protests, "If we try to fight in every revolution in the world, we never stop," and for this he doesn't want to get involved in even one.

★ **Straw man:** The arguer misrepresents their opponents' view and disproves it, thus allegedly proving the person wrong. Hamilton insists Jefferson wants to give the economy "a sedative," then explains why he's against that.

• *Sui Generis* (or Differance): a postmodern stance that rejects the validity of an analogy because every situation or person is "sui generis" i.e., one of a kind. In "One Last Time," Hamilton protests Washington's retirement with "Your position is so unique." Washington disagrees.

★ **Tautology:** Stating the same thing twice in slightly different wording. Hamilton protests in the first Cabinet Battle, "Welcome to the present, we're running a real nation," which is redundant.

★ **Wishful thinking:** An appeal to emotion where a decision is made according to what people wish was happening, rather than according to evidence. As it turns out in "We Know," Jefferson and his company are not acting according to facts, but to their hope that Hamilton has broken the law.

THEME

The show has several themes – messages for the audience to learn or central ideas.

★ **"Who lives, who dies, who tells our story"**: Miranda explains, channeling Shakespeare, "We strut and fret our hour upon the stage, and how that reverberates is entirely out of our control and entirely in the hands of those who survive us" (*Hamilton: The Revolution* 120). Legacy becomes central as Hamilton craves "Something that's gonna/Outlive me" in "The Room Where It Happens," while Eliza insists they "don't need a legacy" in "That Would Be Enough." Washington fusses over how history judges him and Burr mourns that he's made himself the villain. At the beginning of "The Room Where It Happens," Burr and Hamilton discuss General Mercer, whose death has gotten him a permanent legacy as a street in New York. Finally, Eliza the biographer puts herself back in the story and redeems Hamilton by sharing his papers and insights with the world.

In fact, the show has a larger effect on the Founding Fathers' legacy, as many fans can now picture the Founding Fathers as looking like them. As Elise Goldsberry (Angelica Schuyler) explains of her six-year-old son: "These characters are what he's going to think of when he thinks about George Washington and Thomas Jefferson. He will be so surprised when someone hands him a book someday, and he sees pictures of them" (James).

★ **"You will never be satisfied"**: Burr, Eliza, Angelica, and Hamilton all deal with this struggle. As Hamilton courts Angelica, Burr and Hamilton try different paths to the top, and Eliza tells Hamilton to be satisfied with what he has. After "The Reynolds Pamphlet," Angelica observes that Hamilton will never be satisfied. Washington, however, is, as he resigns the presidency. Hamilton finally offers, "That would be enough" in "It's Quiet Uptown," after all that he's lost. He returns Eliza's long-offered faith and trust by flipping her line, "I'm not afraid/I know who I married." He finds satisfaction, though it's almost too late for him. Meanwhile, quiet, sweet Eliza lives for fifty years more and finds new ambitious projects like starting an orphanage…so many projects that she seems to have developed her husband's ambition and declares of her time, "It's not enough." It seems she's the one who's' not satisfied in the end.

★ **"The world was big enough…"**: Burr and Hamilton go from friends to rivals to deadly enemies. Each time they meet, they start their conversation with "Aaron Burr, Sir," (or variants on this) and comparing how their life philosophies are going. In "The Story of Tonight (Reprise)" each wants what the other has and can't understand the other's dissatisfaction. By the end, Hamilton has adopted Burr's "talk less" strategy to compromise with Jefferson, and Burr has started rousing the people as he campaigns for president. Thus, as happens in *Wicked*, their friendship and rivalry has taught each to absorb qualities of the other. At the end, too late, Burr realizes there was room for them both in the world, and by destroying Hamilton, he has destroyed himself.

★ **"Raise a glass to the four of us"**: Genuine friendship follows Hamilton with his team of Laurens, Mulligan, and Lafayette, and Washington adopts him as a surrogate son. Angelica's sister love for Eliza (and also Hamilton) takes precedence over romantic love. All these relationships are treated as precious in the show. Of course, there's also romance, as Hamilton and Eliza's love starts with a perfect moment at the ball, then is complicated by Angelica and Maria in their love triangle. Meanwhile, Angelica wonders several times how much loyalty to her sister should rule over love, and Jefferson taunts Hamilton for not standing by Lafayette. Burr and Hamilton's own friendship strains and shatters, emphasizing that not all relationships can last.

★ **"You will come of age with our young nation"**: Fathers and sons are linked with the new country and revolution as well as the men's strategies and motivations: not just Hamilton's paternal relationship with Washington and his son Philip, but also Burr's struggle with his grandfather's and parents' legacy and what they made him. More, there are nods to God the father, and the concept of Founding Fathers with their legacy.

★ **"Let me tell you what I wish I'd known"**: The Founding Fathers are not infallible. Washington gives up on freeing the slaves and tells Hamilton of mistakes on his first campaign. Hamilton blows up his own life with a sex scandal, and Jefferson, Madison, and Burr put their animosity for Hamilton before the country. All this makes them appear people, not perfect images.

★ **"Immigrants: We get the job done"**: In this success story, a young immigrant arrives in America and makes his mark in American politics. Further, the cast are specifically played by minorities:

> Imagine a Broadway stage where the only white featured lead is King George III, the one common enemy of everyone onstage telling this story about the struggle to first found and then succeed in America. None of them are dressed as lions, and that you're not sitting through yet another iteration of *A Raisin in the Sun* to find some diversity onstage — *Hamilton* is new, fresh and original and, despite the fact that it's set over two hundred years ago, it sounds decidedly like today. (James)

These casting choices emphasize that America was

founded by people who, like many minorities today, felt disempowered by their government.

> Meanwhile, Hamilton's immigrant status, a source of celebration in Act I as Hamilton fights for the land of opportunity, becomes an insult. Jefferson and Madison sneer that "this immigrant isn't somebody we chose." Burr contrasts Hamilton with these smug politicians, quipping, "What happens when two Virginians and an immigrant walk into a room?" Burr argues in the Reynolds Affair that Hamilton will be condemned even more for being an "immigrant embezzling our government funds." Thus as John Adams labels him a "Creole bastard" and Burr calls him an "immigrant bastard," his origins become nasty insults. (Frankel)

These added challenges for the hero remind viewers all immigrants must contend with today.

★ **"Tomorrow there'll be more of us"**: Hamilton's optimism stretches through the narrative, especially after having experienced the horrors of disaster and death. Despite the chaos and loss of his childhood, he believes in boldness and builds a nation through his determination. He truly believes in America, and creates a stronger country.

★ **"I put myself back in the narrative"**: Women like Eliza are cultural guardians, Founding Mothers as important to history as the Fathers, even when they take a backseat to their more famous counterparts. "Who Lives, Who Dies, Who Tells Your Story" emphasizes this, and Ron Chernow opens the Hamilton biography with a prologue showing aging Eliza Hamilton in the 1850s, showing the souvenirs of her life. As she tells the story of her dear husband, she keeps his legacy alive.

MOTIFS

Unlike a theme, a motif need not have a message; sometimes it's just a repeated image. Many concepts and words echo through the many songs: immigrants, one's "shot," writing, "Talk less, smile more." Most of these come with their own musical arcs. "Hey" often appears in moments of flirtation. There are other larger categories:

★ **Lack of understanding:** Burr's protests about "How" and "Why" this immigrant upstart rises so fast suggest his utter bewilderment. Hamilton doesn't fathom Burr either, as he tells him, "I will never understand you" in "The Story of Tonight" (Reprise), and in "Non-Stop," Hamilton protests, "I don't understand how you stand to the side."

★ **Rising and falling**: As Hamilton struggles to make something of himself and also start a revolution in "My Shot," cries of "Rise up!" work for both, as does "Raise a glass to freedom." In "Aaron Burr, Sir" and "The Room Where It Happens," Hamilton contrasts this imagery with Burr's path from success into infamy when he asks Burr: "If you stand for nothing, Burr, what do you fall for?" As Act I ends, Hamilton has completed his "rise to the top" but Burr warns him that his pride goeth before the fall. The spinning turntable echoes the rise and fall as well. As Hamilton dies, he cries "Rise up, Rise up!" circling back to his beginning ambition but suggesting now he's going to heaven. Burr, however, falls permanently from political grace.

★ **Eyes:** Angelica and Eliza both admire Alexander's beautiful eyes. Of course, Washington reminds Hamilton repeatedly, "History has its eyes on you." Jefferson, Madison, and Burr don't trust Hamilton's deceptive eyes in "Washington On Your Side." Dueling participants "Look 'em in the eye, aim no higher." In "Hurricane," Hamilton is trapped in the "eye of the storm," and he recalls that his neighbors had their eyes on him. Alexander's final verse says "Eyes up!" as he looks towards heaven. After this, Eliza sees Alexander in the eyes of the orphans she helped raise after his passing, framing their relationship.

★ **Death:** Hamilton tells Burr and Lafayette, "I'll see you on the other side" in Act I, emphasizing the war as a great divide. This sets up his death scene – the greatest "other side." Death frames the story as the first number lists the deaths that have set him on his path – his mother's, his cousin's. Hamilton also says, "I imagine death so much it feels more like a memory" as early as "My Shot" before he decides to join the Revolution, setting up another arc phrase. As Miranda adds, "In this verse he goes from nihilism to a list of what needs to be done to hope towards tomorrow, and he takes himself there through one uninterrupted train of thought" (*Hamilton: The Revolution* 27). He repeats this in "Yorktown" and as he dies, emphasizing his brushes with mortality. One of Hamilton's motifs is running out of time, a line in "Non-Stop," repeated in "Best of Wives, Best of Women" when he actually is. In his death scene, he adds, "I'm running out of time. I'm running and my time's up…." A clock chimes and all goes silent.

★ **Blended genres:** Modern slang with old-fashioned expressions. Rap and hip-hop with a waltz ball. Military coats and microphones. And yet, it all works.

★ **Waiting:** Burr has a constant motif of waiting, especially in "Wait for it." During the war, Eliza waits at home, the country waits to see who's won at Yorktown. Hamilton doesn't wait, but tells others to, with his repeated line "Just you wait." In "The Room Where it Happens," Hamilton warns Burr, "You get love for it, you get hate for it/You get nothing if you wait for it." They contrast as Hamilton seizes his dreams.

* **Religion:** "Wait for It" has Burr considering how "the sinners and the saints" are treated the same, until he gives in to evil. As Act I ends, Hamilton has completed his "rise to the top" but Burr warns him that his pride goeth before the fall, a Bible quote that proves prophetic.

> Hamilton's literal prayer, for the strength to resist temptation, fails, as he soon gives into Maria: "Lord, show me how to say no to this/I don't know how to say no to this/Cuz the situation's helpless/And her body's screaming, 'Hell, yes'" ("Say No to This"). The antithesis of "Lord" and "Hell" side by side suggest he's teetering on the brink...and soon succumbs. God is also invoked in a scene of sin, not selflessness, adding to the inappropriateness of only turning to God so Hamilton can resist sex. It's no wonder his appeal fails. (Frankel)

Hamilton's final "Rise up, rise up!" suggests heaven, as his friends look down from above.

* **Chess:** The chess metaphors in Act I are associated with the war and include "Knight takes rook, but look" and "We snatch a stalemate from the jaws of defeat." In Act II, war turns to political intrigue with "The pieces that are sacrificed in every game of chess" and "A game of chess, where France is queen-and kingless." The literal battle becomes a figurative one, but Hamilton never stops strategizing.

* **Cycles:** These are a strong motif, reflected in the turntable. Important moments, like ball, duel, and death all swirl as does Hamilton's frantic writing in "Non-Stop" and his desperation in "Hurricane." Cycles continue on a large scale as the American Revolution sparks the French one, and election follows election. Set designer David Korins liked the cinematic aspects of the circular concept:

> It's a sweeping epic, storytelling tool and the show is so epic in scale that when I pitched it to the director and

the choreographer, I actually wrote out several different beats of the show where I imagined we could use this kind of swirling movement. You can also use it like a treadmill; there are many applications of this thing. This swirling movement is really important to the storytelling. (Eddy)

★ There are also musical motifs, as they're called, when phrases, especially names, all come with their own snippet of music. These include "Alexander Hamilton," "Aaron Burr, Sir," "Angelica," "Eliza," "and Peggy."

ALLEGORY

This is a story-length metaphor, in which the entire work mirrors a situation in history, work of literature, etc. Hamilton *as an entire work certainly could be a metaphor for a few circumstances:*

★ **Lin-Manuel Miranda's life:** The story begins with Hamilton insisting he's going to write his way to fame and fortune. "And if that sounds very much like the promise of a young playwright to himself, a goad to ambition and purpose, it should. There's as much Hamilton in Miranda as there is Miranda in Hamilton" (Maggregor). Indeed, *Hamilton* is the story of Lin-Manuel Miranda and his family. As the creator reveals: "My father came here the same age as Hamilton…he came with a full ride for NYU post-doc…didn't speak English" ("Hamilton: A Founding Father"). He recast the Founding Fathers as Black and Latino to look like himself and his fellow actors from *In the Heights*. "This is the story of America then told by America now. It looks like America now," Miranda explains ("Hamilton: A Founding Father"). As he adds:

I fell in love with Chernow's version of Hamilton. I recognized the relentlessness. I recognized the self-destructiveness. I recognize the "no one in the room's realized it yet, but I'm the smartest guy in here" of Hamilton, that energy. I went to a gifted school and I know that kid. And so I fell in love with his version of history, and seeing American history through his eyes made me see it in a totally different way. (Evans)

★ **Macbeth:** The minute Hamilton says "Macbeth" (a play that's actually famous in theater for being cursed – so much that one mustn't same the name unless performing it), all of his decisions have disastrous consequences. He quotes from the play with "Tomorrow and Tomorrow and Tomorrow" while corresponding with Angelica and then protests, "They think me Macbeth, and ambition is my folly" and adds that Jefferson is his nemesis Macduff. Just as the song ends, he causes his own downfall through trying to take more than honor entitles him to (through the Reynolds Affair), causing his own downfall like Macbeth himself. Macbeth, dreaming of greatness, kills his own king, then several others to cover up the crime. At last, these murders make Macduff his great nemesis, all because Macbeth killed Macduff's family while trying to prevent this very downfall. Meanwhile, Hamilton finds himself entranced by Maria Reynolds and breaks his own oaths to his wife. Hiding what he's done by submitting to blackmail, then trying to avoid his fall by making matters worse – publishing the Reynolds Pamphlet – dooms his political career and costs him his son.

★ **Religion:** The heavy link between this show and *Jesus Christ Superstar* is echoed in the religious allegory. Hamilton and Burr are Jesus and Judas or God and Lucifer – in both cases, beginning as beloved allies, but one travels towards goodness and the other, evil and betrayal. At "A Winter's Ball," Burr says

Hamilton is "seated at the right hand of the Father" casting Hamilton as Jesus and Washington as God in this Bible quote. Hamilton's line about what Burr will "fall for" subtly compares him to Lucifer, ostracized and mistreated until he proudly rebels. Burr's "The Room Where it Happens" is devilish-looking with the purple light, as is Hamilton's descent into sin with Maria all in red. Both have uncomfortable, slippery minor cords. However, Hamilton repents his crime and the angelic Eliza all in white finally forgives him. Burr, however, commits to greed and ambition. Burr then directly betrays Hamilton by taking his father-in-law's senate seat. At last, he shoots Hamilton, committing an illegal act that in fact dooms him. Judas betrays Jesus and Lucifer betrays God; thus both become infamous forever and lose all claim to goodness. Burr's final song bitterly reflects on how he's become a "villain" for all time through his act.

★ **Modern Politics:** Many detected commentary on modern Washington DC as politicians endlessly debate, with savage scandals and cruel tricks. Miranda quipped on SNL during the build up to the 2016 presidential election, "It's such a nice escape from all the craziness in our world right now. It's about two famous New York politicians locked in a dirty, ugly, mud-slinging political campaign—escapism!" In fact, the start of partisanship and campaigning appear along with the founding of the nation.

Obama, a huge fan, saw the show several times after Miranda tested out the original rap at the White House. Obama says of it, "Part of what's so powerful about this performance is it reminds us of the vital, crazy kinetic energy that's at the heart of America – that people who have a vision and a set of ideals can transform the world" (*Hamilton: The Revolution* 284). When he invited the cast to the White House, he compared his job with the fictional characters as he spoke about the show's impact. As he added on another occasion:

> And in the Hamilton that Lin-Manuel and his incredible cast and crew bring to life—a man who is "just like his country, young, scrappy, and hungry"—[laughter]—we recognize the improbable story of America and the spirit that has sustained our Nation for over 240 years. Now, in this telling, rap is the language of revolution. Hip-hop is the backbeat. In each brilliantly crafted song, we hear the debates that shaped our Nation, and we hear the debates that are still shaping our Nation. We feel the fierce, youthful energy that animated the men and women of Hamilton's generation. And with a cast as diverse as America itself, including the outstandingly talented women, the show reminds us that this Nation was built by more than just a few great men and that it is an inheritance that belongs to all of us. (Obama)

Miranda started writing this show in 2009, as the modern-day Tea Party movement was taking off. He comments:

> Well, specifically, having the Founding Fathers look like America today strikes me as so radical. And it made me think of some of the Tea Party rhetoric, of how these conservatives were saying, "We need to take our country back." And to me, this show felt like it was saying, "No, you're not taking the country back, and in fact, we're part of the whole history of this country, even going back to the puffy shirts and the tricorn hats." I guess the direct line I can pull on the most is between Hamilton's life story and the immigrant narrative in our country. The fact that immigrants have to work twice as hard just to get here, but that also, at some point, it's going to be thrown in your face as a negative. In Hamilton's case, it was Jefferson and Madison writing basically the same things you would hear about Obama during election cycles: "How do we really know where he's from?"
> Right. (Binelli)

Further, as Kendra James explains in her essay, "Race, Immigration, and Hamilton: The Relevance of Lin-

Manuel Miranda's New Musical":

> It's the urgency to force change – the kind of urgency that has prompted the BLM protests, and interrupted presidential campaign stops, and inspired constant chatter on social media platforms – that Miranda captures perfectly at the end of Act 1 in "Non-Stop." I've listened to *Hamilton* around twenty times since last Monday, so it wasn't a coincidence that I was listening to "Non-Stop" when Shaun King recently detailed the shooting of Jeremy Mcdole by Delaware police on Twitter. Everyday acts of injustice like this give Black Lives Matter (*"Scratch that / this is not a moment, it's the movement"*) its urgency, which Miranda captures in lyrics… It's the same urgency I feel when I see, almost daily, new reports of police brutality towards people of color. I do feel like we might be running out of time

The first Republican Presidential debate for the 2016 presidential campaign aired during Hamilton's opening night, and from then on the show remained tied to the Donald Trump/Hillary Clinton presidential election of 2016. Trump's campaign was anti-immigrant, providing a counterpoint with the show. Miranda adds:

> The fights we're having right now politically are the same fights we've been having since six months after we became a country: states' rights versus national rights, foreign intervention versus how we treat our own people and the rights we have. The original sin of slavery and its repercussions; the original sins of, "Oh, we said everyone could have guns and now everyone has guns" – that's all still here and we're going to be reckoning with it all as long as we're a country. It's *MSNBC* and *Fox News* instead of Hamilton and Jefferson, and the polarities have flipped several times, but we're always going to be having these struggles. We will have periods of anger, and we will have periods of bloodshed, but hopefully we'll take more steps forward than we take back. (DiGiacomo)

Only a week after the election, Vice President-elect Mike Pence, who had passed harsh anti-gay legislation and had campaigned on an anti-immigrant platform, attended the show. Many in the crowd booed him and cheered remarkably long at "Immigrants/We get the job done!" At the end, the cast, all of whom had gay or immigrant friends or family, addressed him. Brandon Dixon, who played Aaron Burr, began the short prepared statement by thanking Pence for attending the play and saying, "We hope you will hear us out."

"We, sir – we are the diverse America who are alarmed and anxious that your new administration will not protect us, our planet, our children, our parents, or defend us and uphold our inalienable rights," Dixon said. "We truly hope that this show has inspired you to uphold our American values and to work on behalf of all of us." (Bradner)

Thus the show crossed borders to affect the day's politics instead of just mirroring them. Trump tweeted his irritation at this speech ("The Theater must always be a safe and special place. The cast of Hamilton was very rude last night to a very good man, Mike Pence. Apologize!"), and much of America took sides in a debate about the actors' speaking out…for a few days, at least. Still, the show remained tied to politics of the day as well as to those of centuries past.

ALLUSION

An allusion is a reference to another work (generally brief – a sustained one through the show is considered allegory). Some are deliberate little winks, today often called "Easter eggs" from the computer game term. Others are more sweeping homages, nodding to the shows that inspired this one. Greek mythology and the Bible (seen here) are popular, as is history, which obviously shows up. Miranda doesn't reference Shakespeare or literature much here, preferring modern musicals, rap, hip-hop, and pop culture.

★ "The four grandparents of the show," director Tommy Kail says, "are *Sweeney Todd, Jesus Christ Superstar, Evita,* and *Gypsy.*" Kail explains, "*Gypsy* and *Sweeney* are the story of monsters…they're both about somebody who has already been judged by history, but the shows still creates mystery about why the monsters do what they do. *Evita* and *Jesus Christ Superstar* shows that music could lead the way" – they started as concept albums and were virtually sung through (*Hamilton: The Revolution,* 159). Both inspired the structure of the show, in which the antihero narrator tells the story of the life of his nemesis, the tragic protagonist. (This also appears in *Wicked.*)

★ From the musical *Gypsy,* Hamilton is the main character, stage mom Rose. "Brash and politically insensitive, arrogant and brilliant, sometimes right but never in doubt," he builds a great career then implodes it (Viertel 266).

★ On the first page of the libretto, Lin-Manuel explains that the opening number of *Hamilton* – initially a monologue for Aaron Burr and the first song written – "owes a debt to the prologue of *Sweeney Todd:* All our characters set the stage for our main man's entrance." In this show, the hero, now dead, rises from the grave to tell his own story as a show-length flashback, a structure that inspired Miranda. The opening number "sets the style, the tone (unique as it is) and the point of view of the show perfectly (complete with the information that the hero will be dead at the final blackout)" (Viertel 60).

★ "The hip-hop narrative is writing your way out of your circumstances" Miranda explains ("Hamilton: A Founding Father"). Thus his character nods to hip-hop narratives from the start.

★ Burr's opening lines sound like parts of "The Message" by Grandmaster Flash and the Furious Five.

★ "The ten-dollar founding father" references, unusually, American currency. Hamilton was nearly removed from the bill around this time, and the show's popularity actually kept him on it.

★ The opening number has the call-and-response of "What's your name?" – a mode familiar from hits from everyone from Snoop Dogg to DMX to Rihanna and Drake.

★ "Alexander Hamilton" offers the line "America sings for you," which may nod to "I Hear America Singing," a poem from Whitman's *Leaves of Grass*.

★ The repeated chorus of "New York, New York!" (in "Alexander Hamilton" and, later, "The Schuyler Sisters") echoes other songs about the city, especially "Empire State of Mind."

★ On the NYC subway system, this exact intonation of "What time is it?" "SHOWTIME!" is used by performers about to dance in the middle of the moving train. "Get on the Mic" by Beastie Boys echoes the tune and mood of the men's introductions here.

★ In "My Shot," Lafayette describes himself as Lancelot, and his first lines echo Lancelot's "C'Est Moi" from *Camelot* (the musical) when he says, "Who's the best?/C'est moi!" The mythic Lancelot actually brings down Arthur and Camelot, which may nod to Lafayette's later role as the adversary Jefferson.

★ "I'm John Laurens in the place to be" is "a love letter to old school hip-hop" and a staple of rap (*Hamilton: The Revolution* 25). Miranda often used a similar opening in his own raps.

★ In the same introduction song, Mulligan's "Brrrrah! Brrrah!" mimics a rapidly firing gun – a staple of hip-hop songs.

★ Hamilton's "I'm a diamond in the rough" nods to *Aladdin*, a Disney film and also a musical.

★ "Only 19, but my mind is old(er)" is a quote from Mobb Deep's "Shook Ones Pt II." In the line there's also a Mobb Deep shrill tone hip-hop fans recognize. There's also a line from the musical *Rent* saying "I'm 19, but old for my age..."

★ The way Hamilton spells out his name is a reference to how The Notorious Big does it in "Going Back to Cali."

★ A reference to Tupac's "Holler If Ya Hear Me" appears with "I gotta holler just to be heard."

★ Big Pun likes a string of rhymes and Miranda uses those too with lines like "between all the bleedin' 'n fightin'/I've been readin' 'n writin'."

★ The refrain borrows from the words of Eminem's "Lose Yourself," while the snare drum "double bounce" suggests a soldier's call to arms.

★ Laurens's "on a stallion/with the first black battalion" echoes "...or retalion'/all fine young black females stallions" from Juvenile's "400 Degreez."

★ "You've got to be carefully taught" nods to the song of that name from the musical *South Pacific*. Burr gets in another in the same rhyme as he urges his rebel colleagues: "The situation is fraught" from *A Funny Thing Happened on the Way to the Forum*.

★ Hamilton offers a Biblical allusion, comparing his countrymen's need to leave England and Moses leading the slaves out of Egypt: "We roll like Moses, claimin' our promised land."

★ Historical allegory is constant – many songs paraphrase or quote real-life documents, especially "A Farmer Refuted," "Right-Hand Man," "One Last Time" and "The Reynolds Pamphlet." In "The Schuyler Sisters," Angelica mentions reading *Common Sense* by Thomas Paine, and quotes the Declaration of Independence.

★ "The Story of Tonight" is written in the style of "Drink with Me" from *Les Misérables*, in which the friends sing an ode to their friendship before the rebellion that may kill them all. This was Miranda's first musical, which made an enormous impression.

★ "The Schuyler Sisters" sounds like Destiny's Child, a deliberate homage after Miranda and musical director Alex Lacamoire heard the actresses singing together in this style and encouraged them to keep harmonizing.

★ Miranda calls Burr's "Excuse me, miss, I know it's not funny/But your perfume smells like your daddy's got money" in "The Schuyler Sisters" "our little Jay Z/Pharrel homage" (*Hamilton: The Revolution* 44).

★ Burr's meeting with the Schuyler sisters is a nod to The Lovin' Spoonful's "Summer in the City," also echoed in "Say No to This."

★ The phrase "Looking for a mind at work" is from *The West Wing,* which Miranda enjoys. Later there's another *West Wing* line – "Come home at the end of the day."

★ Angelica's intonation on the word "insane" nods to Nicki Minaj's verse in Kanye West's "Monster."

★ All three King George songs evoke the Beatles, echoing the melodies of "Penny Lane," "With a Little Help From My Friends," "Getting Better," and "For the Benefit of Mr Kite." The line "Everybody!" at the end of "You'll be Back" nods to John Lennon in "All You Need Is Love."

★ "Right Hand Man" has the ensemble calling "What" "in what sounds like a very precise imitation of one of DMX's signature ad libs in songs like "Party Up in Here" (Wickman). The repeating "Boom goes the cannon" is from Busta Rhymes' part in "Scenario." The bass line is influenced by Eminem's "Lose Yourself."

★ Washington's "Now I'm the model of a modern major general" restates the line from the classic musical *The Pirates of Penzance,* as does his alliteration in this scene.

> The section of "Right Hand Man" in which George Washington is courting Hamilton to come work by his side reminded me of "Coming of Age," from Jay Z's debut album, "Reasonable Doubt." It's a back-and-forth between him and a hungry protégé, Memphis Bleek. Jay is looking for an eager student, and I can imagine Bleek coming back at him with Hamilton's refrain: "I am not throwing away my shot." (Tommasini and Caramanica)

★ The ball where Hamilton meets Eliza has some of the men calling out for the "laaaadies" in an echo of the Beastie Boys' "Hey Ladies."

★ "Helpless" echoes Beyonce's "Countdown" – music, rhythm, and words. For its origins, Miranda recalls nineties pop/hip-hop crossovers including Mary J. Blige and Method Man's "I'll Be There for You/ You're All I Need to Get By" and Beyoncé's "Crazy in Love" with a guest verse from Jay Z (*Hamilton: The Revolution* 68). Lacamoire explains, "The Beyoncé reference is 'Stressin'! Blessin'!' sounds like 'Houston rocket!' [in 'Countdown']. We asked the girls to deliver it like that" (Jones).

★ "My heart went boom" in "Helpless" comes from the love ballad "I Saw Her Standing There."

★ Hamilton's own growl in "Helpless" is an homage to JaRule, included because it makes his costar laugh.

★ Though the music of the show is modern rap with R&B and other popular genres, there's a few bars of the most traditional song of all, "The Bridal Chorus," to signal Alexander and Eliza's wedding. In fact, the song is used because it is so easily recognized.

★ In "Satisfied," Angelica gets in a moment of history and nod to the Founding Fathers as she compares her instant connection with Hamilton to Ben Franklin's experiment with lightning.

★ The "takes and it takes and it takes" line in "Wait for It" plays with Job 1:21, in which the beleaguered Job says, "Naked I came from my mother's womb, and naked I will depart. The Lord gave and the Lord has taken away."

★ "Ten Duel Commandments" is one giant reference to "Ten Crack Commandments." Of course, both reference the Biblical Ten Commandments as well. Miranda comments, "It's a song about illegal activity, and how it works. And we're both stealing the structure from Moses" (Mead).

★ In "Stay Alive," Hamilton quips, "Sing a song of Sixpence," a British nursery rhyme. The historical Hamilton might have actually known that one.

★ "Meet Me Inside" repeats the title phrase, apparently inverting a repeated "meet me outside" (with the same rhythm) in DMX's "Party Up in Here."

★ "'Guns and Ships' sounds like a nod to a classic Eminem song as Hamilton, Lafayette, Burr and Washington discuss the war and the effort that goes into fighting one. It's also the speediest record on Broadway with 19 words per second ("Going H.A.M.").

★ "We're in the shit now and somebody's gotta shovel it," Hercules Mulligan says. The mythic Hercules actually did this as one of his famed twelve tasks. With this, there's a mythology allusion. There's also the man's hero name, but that was the name of the real historical figure.

★ The cut song "Valley Forge," (now changed to "Stay Alive"), features the line, "I've seen the best minds of my generation/Waste away on pestilence and starvation," referencing Allen Ginsberg's *Howl*.

★ Busta Rhymes goes from soft to suddenly loud, and "Yorktown" imitates this.

★ "The World Turned Upside Down" is actually a British drinking song sung as the British departed Yorktown. A few of its real lyrics appear. Mary J. Blige's version of "I'm Going Down," with the lyric, "My whole world's turned upside down" also echoes some of the tones.

★ "Yorktown (The World Turned Upside Down)" and "What'd I Miss?" mention "the American experiment," a phase from *Democracy in America* by Alexis de Tocqueville.

★ Hamilton tells the other soldiers, "Through the night, we have one shot to live another day," paralleling a line from the chorus of "Lose Yourself" ("You only get one shot, do not miss your chance to blow").

★ In "Non-Stop," Hamilton nods to philosophers with "If not, then I'll be Socrates/Throwing verbal rocks at these mediocrities."

★ A verse in "Non-Stop" nods to Inspectah Deck's lines in Wu-Tang's "Triumph": "I bomb atomically, Socrates' philosophies and hypotheses/Can't define how I be dropping these mockeries."

★ Several members of the ensemble hold a tabletop for Hamilton to write on in "Non-Stop," nodding to the late-19th-century painting "Cossacks of Saporog Are Drafting a Manifesto" by Russian artist Ilya Repin.

★ This intersection of plotlines and characters, each singing their theme songs as they discover a new world on the edge of war echoes "One Day More" from *Les Miserables,* also the act break song.

★ Jefferson's purple coat evokes Prince. Miranda explains:

> It's about eliminating distance. If your mission is to make a story that happened 200-odd years ago resonate with contemporary audiences, what are the ways in which you can eliminate distance? And, man, does that purple suit with a frilly blouse do that. Just like when we pull out those microphones for that

> Cabinet battle. It's the only anachronistic prop in the
> show. (Binelli)

✴ A bit of the hip-hop classic "The Message" appears in "What'd I Miss."

✴ The brief interlude "No John Trumbull" (cut from the final version of the show) contrasts the famous stately historical painting *Declaration of Independence* with the angry, squabbling reality.

✴ Of course, the rap battles, with speedy, free-flowing insults, certainly spice up the political debate. "The rap battles, I think, are 'you think our country should be like this, our country should be like that,' and if you win, our country goes to ruins" Miranda adds ("Hamilton: A Founding Father").

> A confrontational cadence is the warp and woof of rap.
> Even the most "conscious," constructive, or even
> puckish rappers retain a chip on-the-shoulder tone in
> their delivery (not accidentally termed "spitting" among
> fans). Each rhyme at the end of a line implies a "So,
> there!" Rapping is, to an extent, sport. This works so
> well in Hamilton because most of the characters are
> men in competition. It isn't an accident that two debates
> between Hamilton and Jefferson, amenable to
> recasting as rap battles, are among the high points of
> the show. But argument, topping, and display are only
> one part of being human—or of being a character in a
> musical. (McWhorter 51)

✴ The rap battle opens with its moderator, George Washington, introducing the event: "Ladies and gentlemen, you could've been anywhere in the world tonight, but you're here with us in New York City!" This echoes Jay Z's "Izzo (H.O.V.A.)." "Set to a Harlem Shake-ready beat, the disagreement finds George Washington trying to moderate and diffuse tensions between the two" ("Going H.A.M."). Hamilton grins triumphantly as he dances about, taking a fundamental joy in the competition – another hallmark of rap battles.

★ Thomas Jefferson begins his second verse with an homage to Grandmaster Flash's landmark single "The Message." He tells Hamilton he doesn't have the votes, he adds a little "ah ha ha ha," and then smirks, "Such a blunder/Sometimes it makes me wonder/why I even bring the thunder." In "The Message," the refrain is "It's like a jungle/Sometimes it makes me wonder/How I keep from going under/Ah ha ha ha." Musical director Alex Lacamoire explained:

> That first rap battle, it's more old-school. He even does that Grandmaster Flash reference: "a-ha-ha-ha-ha." Whereas the second one just has the cool Neptunes, Pharrell vibe to it. The bass is very round, it doesn't have a lot of bite to it, and the drums are super Neptunes-y, like, *boom-kat, boom-ta-tic-cacko!* (Jones)

★ Angelica's lines in "Take a Break:" "I noticed a comma in the middle of a phrase/It changed the meaning. Did you intend this?" was a historic tease she and Alexander used. However, it's also from *The West Wing*, which discusses a comma or a "smudge of justice" that could change the meaning of the Takings Clause in the 5th Amendment.

★ The cheating song "Say No to This" starts with a quote from LL Cool J's "I Need Love."

★ Hamilton invokes "The Last Five Years," which also describes infidelity, when he pays off Reynolds, telling him, "Nobody needs to know." The music is similar too.

★ In the second cabinet battle, there's Biggie reference from "Juicy," with Jefferson's "And if you don't know, now you know, Mr. President."

★ "The Room Where It Happens" echoes "Somewhere in a Tree," from Stephen Sondheim's *Pacific Overtures* score with a sinister jazz or blues feel.

★ "The Room Where It Happens" may be another West Wing reference as Sam comments of the Oval Office, "I've got to get back in there. That's where it's happening." In another episode, Leo comments, "There are two things in the world you never want to let people see how you make 'em – laws and sausages," creating the analogy of making policy and making sausage – both behind closed doors. This comes from Otto von Bismarck's quote "Laws are like sausages, it is better not to see them being made."

★ Hamilton quotes St. Augustine when he says, "Hate the sin, love the sinner."

★ The line "two Virginians and an immigrant walk into a room" is a classic "walk into a bar" joke.

★ "In God we trust" appears – it's the motto of the United States.

★ "Dark as a tomb where it happens" references the resurrection of Jesus.

★ "Click boom and it happens" nods to "Click Click Boom" by Saliva.

★ "Washington on your Side" includes the phrase "Follow the money" from *All the President's Men*.

★ Washington quotes from the historic Washington's favorite Bible verse in "One Last Time": "Everyone shall sit under their own vine and fig tree/And no one shall make them afraid."

★ will.i.am's "Yes We Can," created for Barack Obama's presidential campaign in 2008, intertwines one character's speaking and one singing, as appears in "One Last Time."

★ In "The Adams Administration," "Sit down, John," shares tune and words with the opening number of the musical *1776*. The profanities are closer to the beginning quote of Tupac Shakur's "Hit 'Em Up."

The cut line "They were callin' you a dick back in '76" is also a *1776* reference.

★ In "We Know," "Unless..." is a reference to *My Brother, My Brother and Me.*

★ In "Burn," Angelica compares Hamilton to Icarus, the mythological hero who was so ambitious he flew too high and died.

★ "It's Quiet Uptown" is reminiscent of "Biggie's 'Suicidal Thoughts,' still one of the most chilling hip-hop songs of all time," as the hero and heroine "confront [their] own mortality [and] end up exhausted, frayed, desperate" (Tommasini and Caramanica).

★ Burr's "I look back on where I failed" in "Your Obedient Servant" is an homage to Javert's "I am reaching, but I fall" from *Les Miserables.*

★ "An itemized list of 30 years of disagreements" appears in *Parks and Recreation.*

★ Burr's line and song title that "The World was Wide Enough" alludes to a comment Burr made decades later. He had two prized books – the one by the philosopher Voltaire recommended a ruthless response to insults. The other was the satirical *Tristam Shandy* by Lawrence Stern, in which a man is about to kill a fly, but stops, deciding the world is large enough for them both. Burr said, "If I had read more Stern and less Voltaire, perhaps I would have realized that the world was large enough for both Hamilton and me" ("The Duel").

★ Ending a musical with someone other than the protagonist is unusual, but Miranda felt that another musical, in this case, *Caroline or Change,* gave him permission (*Hamilton: The Revolution* 280).

FORESHADOWING

Foreshadowing is to hint at or set up things to come in a story

★ Of course, the opening number reveals numerous characters and events from the entire musical: Hamilton with his friends, enemies, family, and the events of the show, including how it will end.

★ Burr and Hamilton, who begin as friends, drop hints of a darker future, like Burr's "fools who run their mouths off wind up dead." Also, the next person to respond here is Laurens, who does in fact die. In "Non-Stop," Burr says of Hamilton, "Soon that attitude may be your doom." There's a similar exchange in "The Room Where It Happens":

> Burr: The Mercer legacy is secure
> Hamilton: Sure.
> Burr: And all he had to do was die.
> Hamilton: That's a lot less work.
> Burr: We oughta give it a try.
> Hamilton: Ha!

★ Hamilton's line "I imagine death so much it feels like a memory" is first heard in "My Shot," then again in the opening line of "Yorktown," and finally in his death scene. He sees it coming from the start.

★ "Look around at how lucky we are to be alive right now" in "The Schuyler Sisters" is sung happily and sincerely by the eager sisters, then the line appears from a high-spirited pregnant Eliza in "That Would Be Enough." In "Non-Stop" Hamilton uses Eliza's line against her to justify leaving the family, tossing back the line she used about their separation previously. It appears again, in a dark reprise in "It's Quiet Uptown." With this, the luck slowly deteriorates.

★ During "A Winter's Ball," Angelica continues watching Hamilton after they flirt. "Satisfied" explains what was really going on here.

★ Eliza's happy love for Hamilton appears in the word and song "Helpless," but it's less happy when he chooses public service over her. She actually ends up helpless in their relationship. When he begins an affair, he uses the word, and finally Eliza reclaims her power in "Burn," getting past the word.

★ Eliza's delighted "I do" at the beginning of "Helpless" echoes her upcoming marriage to Hamilton by the song's end.

★ Angelica adds to her sister, "I'm just sayin', if you really loved me, you would share him" (a historical quip in her letters), which sets up the coming love triangle.

★ Philip Schuyler's "Be true" may imply he already knows or suspects Hamilton's wandering eye.

★ The "Ten Duel Commandments" is like a practice round for dueling before the more serious duels that follow. Burr and Hamilton, the seconds, meet on the field and debate the logic of settling arguments this way, a debate that pays out at the end.

★ Hamilton promises Lafayette before the Battle of Yorktown that the Americans will aid the French in their own Revolution. Lafayette abruptly changes the subject and tells Hamilton to go lead his men. Perhaps Lafayette doesn't think America will be able to aid them, which ends up being what happens in the second Cabinet Battle.

★ Hamilton refuses to throw away his shot (as in, his chance), and tells Laurens the same, ironically that he shouldn't throw away his by shooting someone. While Alexander is singing "I am not throwing away my shot" during "Non-Stop" the chorus warningly sings "Just you wait." There's also his son's duel, where he *does* advise him to throw away his shot, all before he attempts to delope during his duel with Burr. "Wait For It" also echoes after Burr's song, when Hamilton taunts Burr in "The Room Where It Happens" and, heartbreakingly Burr screams "Wait!" too late in their duel.

★ The ensemble member who plays the Bullet at the musical's end offers foreshadowing from the beginning. Ariana DeBose, the original Bullet (identifiable by a poof of curls atop her head), said, "I always know I'm aiming for him—even if the rest of the ensemble members don't. So even if I'm just a lady in a ball gown at a party, there's still a part of my character that knows that *that* moment is going to come" (Corde). In "My Shot," she unfreezes last during the "I imagine death so much it feels more like a memory" monologue. She stands beside Hamilton in "Ten Duel Commandants" at numbers six through seven, and he looks at her, anticipating the show's final duel as he brushes death.

★ When Eliza greets him in "That Would Be Enough," she's standing by the stone bench signifying the exterior of their house. It's gravelike, foreshadowing "Burn," and the deaths to follow.

★ "What Comes Next" has King George emphasize that the Americans will have a difficult time leading. This perfectly sets up Act II.

★ Chekhov's Gun: Chekhov, the great Russian playwrite, said "If in the first act you have hung a pistol on the wall, then in the following one it should be fired." Many writers insist the reverse is true as well – if a gun will be fired, it should first appear in the background. In the show, the dueling pistols that kill Hamilton's son and then Hamilton himself are hanging on the wall through the entire second act. Not only does the set designer show awareness of this concept, but the fact that they're literally guns makes a joke for those in the know.

★ Hamilton sings "You knock me down, I fall apart" in "Dear Theodosia," as Hamilton expresses his love for his son, but the phrase returns in "It's Quiet

Uptown," when Hamilton is more literally devastated by Philip's death. The "Dear Theodosia" line "someday you'll blow us all away" appears later as the title and chorus of the song where Philip gets into a deadly duel.

★ Philip's counting and musical motif in his piano practice echoes the "Ten Duel Commandments," in which he dies.

★ In a cut song, Eliza sings "Let it Go" directly after Burr takes the senate seat, encouraging Hamilton not to publish scathing letters. Hamilton also considers writing angry letters in "One Last Time," and actually publishes them in "The Adams Administration" – setting up this moment as well as the Reynolds scandal. Eliza's line "You don't have to bring a gun to a knife fight" also foreshadows the end.

★ In the second Cabinet Battle, Jefferson wants to "shoot" Hamilton with information, anticipating his final fate.

★ Burr's ambition for "the room where it happens," the room where the meeting deciding the location of the nation's capital was held, changes to a desire for the presidency, described with the same phrase.

METAFICTION

Self-aware fiction that comments on itself, addresses the audience, or otherwise calls attention to being fictional. This is often just clever and fun, though sometimes it criticizes or questions the art form.

★ Hamilton, like Miranda, writes his way out of his circumstances and into fame, beginning with his opening number. Thus it becomes a story about writing.

★ The prologue and epilogue, explaining why the main story is being told and what will happen in it, call attention to its fictional nature by analyzing the story itself.

★ The cast of Black, Latina, and Asian American leads modernizes the story, since it's one of immigrants, cast with those who look like today's minorities. This "emphasizes not only the reality of who actually built and expanded America" (James) and also reminds the audience this is fictional.

★ Stage directions abound, from Hamilton's friends and enemies "waiting in the wings for you" and "America sings for you" in the opening number to Hamilton directing himself with "Enter, Me" in "My Shot."

★ "Just you wait" works as commentary on his life as well as an instruction to the audience.

★ Since Burr serves as narrator of the show, he often addresses the audience with rhetorical questions or foreshadowing, even using the label "you.' During "Say No To This" he explains why he turns over the narrative to Alexander.

★ Changing coats onstage suggests putting on a costume for a new role, calling attention to the play again.

★ Lafayette, Laurens, and Mulligan burst in crying "Show time!" then encourage Burr to join in in their rap circle by asking him to "give us a verse," as in, join in with their song. All this is describing what's actually happening here.

★ Lafayette says "Wow" in "My Shot," apparently impressed with either Hercules's sexual exploits or perhaps his complex rhyming.

★ The chorus of "They'll tell the story of tonight" reminds the audience they're watching a story and shows how it will impact history.

★ Hamilton angrily tells Seabury not to change the song's key while they're arguing.

★ In King George's first song, he cries "Everybody!" inviting the audience to join in too.

★ Burr tells the audience that Martha Washington named her tomcat after Alexander; Hamilton (or perhaps Lin-Manuel Miranda, who's playing him), breaks from what he's doing to tell the audience "that's true."

★ "The moment you've been waiting for!" Burr says of Washington. Considering Chris Jackson was also one of the more well-known cast members, who'd appeared in *In The Heights,* some audience members would have literally been waiting for his appearance.

★ In "That Would Be Enough," Eliza tells Hamilton, "Let this moment be the first chapter."

★ "History has its eyes on you," a repeated line, reminds viewers that they, the descendants of this story, are watching too. Eliza discusses legacy and how they'll be remembered – the topic of the show and also its result.

★ In the cut "Valley Forge," Washington says they're trapped in a "horror show." It's literally a show of course.

★ In King George's "What Comes Next," "I'm so blue" turns his spotlight blue, reminding viewers they're in a fictional space.

★ "Non-Stop" has Hamilton references the musical with the line "Corruption's such an old song that we can sing along in harmony." He also busies himself writing the speeches he's giving onstage.

★ The song "What'd I Miss" is a nod to the audience, straggling late to their seats after intermission. Also, Madison waves at the audience while Jefferson is introducing his character.

★ Washington opens the first Cabinet Battle with, "Ladies and gentlemen, you coulda been anywhere in the world tonight, but you're here with us in New York City. Are you ready for a cabinet meeting?" This works for the audience onstage and the real audience, who are indeed seeing a cabinet battle on Broadway, New York City.

★ Young Philip writes his own rap, emulating both father and composer.

★ At the end of "I Know Him" after describing how fun the next part of the show will be, the king plonks himself in a chair onstage to watch.

★ Hamilton decides to write his way out yet again, with Reynolds Pamphlet, a long essay explaining the affair. It was "a ninety-five-page booklet: thirty-seven pages of personal confessions, supplemented by fifty-eight pages of letters and affidavits" (Chernow 533).

★ During "The Reynolds Pamphlet," Jefferson and his friends hand copies to everyone, including the King, who's now watching the show, and the conductor in the orchestra pit.

★ In "Burn," Eliza takes charge of the narrative as she burns the letters. Her song focuses on words and writing, calling attention to lyrics like her own with "You and your words flooded my senses/Your sentences left me defenseless/You built me palaces out of paragraphs." In an added level, the man playing her husband not only wrote the letters but the show itself.

★ Philip walks into a play and interrupts it, reminding viewers they're watching a play of their own. Historically Philip actually did interrupt the play *The West Indian* for his duel, paralleling his father's origins (Chernow 651).

★ Dying, Philip recalls of his music, "I would always change the line." This works as commentary on writing and a reflection of Philip's rule-breaking life.

★ Philip, who died at 19, lived through 19 songs. Hamilton died at 47, and the musical has roughly 47 songs, depending how one counts.

★ "The Election of 1800" opens with Jefferson saying, "Can we get back to politics?" and Madison, wiping his eyes after watching the tragedy of Hamilton's son, sniffles and adds "Please?"

★ In his final speech, Hamilton says, "There is no beat, no melody" – literally true.

★ Much of "The World Was Wide Enough," is addressed toward the audience. Burr protests, "They won't teach you this in your classes, but look it up, Hamilton was wearing his glasses" directly to the audience.

★ At the musical's end, Eliza looks out and gasps. She appears to see the audience, revealing how important Hamilton's and her legacy became. In this case, the figure escorting her might be Hamilton, but also perhaps the show's creator Lin-Manuel Miranda, revealing to her the audience she's won over.

CHARACTERS

Many English instructors break down basic types of character, in a tool for analyzing fiction:

★ **Antagonist** (arch-villain, archenemy, enemy, nemesis): The opposition character or obstacle against which the protagonist must contend. This principal enemy changes and defines the hero through their struggle. While Jefferson is Hamilton's main political opponent, his battles with Burr are more personal, finally destroying him. Hamilton defeats Burr in the election with a single sentence and vote: "When all is said and all is done/Jefferson has beliefs. Burr has none." With this, Hamilton forces his final conflict with the unprincipled schemer. Historian Carol Berkin adds: "Even though he disagreed totally with Jefferson, Jefferson at least was interested in trying to do something that would be good for the United States. Burr – Burr was in it for Burr" (*Alexander Hamilton: American Experience*).

* **Anti-Hero:** A protagonist who lacks conventional goodness or isn't very admirable. While Hamilton, despite his mistakes, is more conventionally heroic, Burr – unprincipled and conniving, is sympathetic enough to deserve this label.

* **Character arc:** How the character grows and changes through the story. Hamilton goes from untutored immigrant to soldier, husband, and father to the man who created large sections of the US government.

* **Characterization:** Qualities that make the character more of a person: likes and dislikes, expressions, history, and so forth.

* **Characterization (direct):** The character's words and actions, like Hamilton's affair and his verbal protests that he doesn't want to cheat.

* **Characterization (indirect):** suggested or narrated rather than shown directly. Burr says much of Hamilton, but his questions of how he can gain respect and his protest of why Hamilton wore glasses to their duel are left for the audience to puzzle out.

* **Caricature:** A character who is given a combination of oversimplified and exaggerated characteristics and features for mockery. King George's childishness and obliviousness to what's happening mark him as this.

* **Dynamic/Round:** A dynamic character learns and changes by resolving conflicts or facing a major crisis. These moments are vital to the story and make the audience relate. Hamilton and Burr do this.

* **Fatal Flaw:** The weakness in a character that makes him/her create his/her downfall, like pride or greed. Hamilton's flying into rages and refusing to apologize not only costs him a political career, but also gets him killed when he refuses to apologize to Burr for his comments. Further, "Hurricane" shows how Hamilton's greatest strengths – his honesty and his writing ability – become tragic weaknesses when he

decides to write his way out of his problems, as he always has.

★ **Flat/Static:** A flat character, the opposite of a round character, is notable for one kind of personality trait like always being sour or perky, and doesn't grow and change. These are normally supporting characters. Peggy, the king, and Seabury aren't seen changing.

★ **Foil:** A character (usually the antagonist) whose personal qualities contrast with another character (usually the protagonist). This contrast helps them both to grow as they define themselves by the other. If Hamilton is the protagonist, then Burr is the villain. However, they have strange links during the story – both prodigy orphans, both Revolutionary war heroes, each so envious of what the other has. The pair begin with opposite philosophies as Hamilton is passionate and Burr reserved, but by the end, they've each tried the other's strategies to succeed. Thus knowing each other has transformed each one. Also, while Hamilton dies and is generally viewed as a "hero," thanks to Eliza, Burr for the rest of his life carries the stigma of the killing.

Other foils are suggested by the freedom-craving Lafayette and Hercules Mulligan, each replaced by cautious politicians played by the same actors. These go from Hamilton's best friends to worst enemies. "As Hamilton's friend Hercules Mulligan, Oak [Okieriete Onaodowan] rapped in a booming growl and pretended that he had trouble controlling his powerful limbs; as James Madison, he shrank his 5'11," 235-pound frame, and adopted a nasal voice, diminishing himself to play Jefferson's shy, sickly partner" (*Hamilton: The Revolution*, 148). Daveed Diggs offers a similar contrast, especially as his coat turns from soldier blue to purple velvet:

> Further, Lafayette's loyal determination to make the war succeed then spread freedom to his own country clashes with Jefferson's privileged demands that all of America conform to his view – the gentleman farmer undesirous of a national treasury or slave emancipation. Nonetheless, both are patriots, driven by their conviction and both ardently support the French Revolution. There's extra meaning when Jefferson insists the new country should aid Lafayette, though Hamilton and Washington refuse this last plea from an old friend. (Frankel)

Leaders King George (who's insane and childish) and the serious, stately George Washington are cast in opposition, as their entrance songs appear back to back, with opposite sounds from the king's Beatles-style singalong to Washington's barked commands. A last pair of foils are passionate, clever Angelica and demure, sweet Eliza, Hamilton's brain and Hamilton's heart, who want opposite types of relationships and pursue them. They compare their lives over and over (though Hamilton), while maintaining a devoted friendship.

✴ **Minor characters:** These complement the major characters and move the plot events forward but sometimes don't even have names and don't grow and change. Some in the show, like Eliza's father, are even played by the ensemble.

✴ **Persona:** A character or figurative mask that an actor, writer, or singer takes on in order to perform. Miranda's Hamilton persona drops away in a few moments, as Hamilton or possibly Miranda bursts in with "that's true" over the tomcat story, or he reacts to joy more like Miranda would than Hamilton.

✴ **Protagonist:** The main character with a conflict to resolve. The audience empathizes with him or her and thus commits to the story. Obviously, the title emphasizes this is Hamilton's story.

★ **Sidekick:** Madison accompanies Jefferson to his cabinet battles and backs him up, though he doesn't argue himself. Further, when Jefferson drops his mic in one of the Cabinet Battles, Madison catches it.

★ **Stock:** Stock characters are conventional or stereotypical through repeated use. Such a traditional character as the Temptress or Tyrant (both seen in the show) doesn't need a lot of character building – they enter and are instantly recognizable.

★ **Supporting character:** Non-main character, usually a helper to the hero like Hamilton's group of friends.

★ **Tragic hero:** The hero who is destroyed, most often because of his own actions. Certainly Hamilton's mouth accomplishes this.

★ **Symbolic:** A symbolic character's existence represents some major idea or aspect of society. King George is such a stock tyrant that when he's ridiculous, the show mocks all of tyranny and authoritarian government.

CONFLICT

The problem of the story; what's stopping the protagonist from accomplishing his goal. There are several basic types:

★ **Person vs. Fate/God:** Person's fate is guaranteed, and he/she struggles against it. The opening number establishes that Burr will shoot Hamilton. Thus as the pair become friends and frenemies and then political opponents, the audience is all-too aware of where they're both heading. In the final few songs, Hamilton tries avoiding this fate, squirming and playing with definitions of insult in their letters, then debating whether to fire at the sky in the duel. However, he succumbs to fate in the end.

★ **Person vs. Nature:** The hero must overcome a force of nature and endure. There's little of this in the story, though the cut song "Valley Forge" would have had a touch of survival story.

★ **Person vs. Person:** Characters want opposite things or struggle for the same thing, pitting them against each other. Interpersonal conflict fills the story, especially in Burr and Hamilton's opposition, resulting in their final duel, and Jefferson and Hamilton's cabinet battles in an entire act of clashing. There's also King George versus the Colonists.

★ **Person vs. Self:** The protagonist struggles internally and must overcome his/her own nature to succeed. . "Congratulations," Angelica's cut song, has her say of the disastrous Reynolds Pamphlet: "Y'know, you're the only enemy you ever seem to lose to!" (Dreamcatcher). Hamilton self-sabotages in the second act, and Burr hesitates, each becoming his own worst enemy. However, in their final duel, they go too far the other way, as Hamilton is cautious and Burr precipitous, destroying them both. Angelica likewise has an enormous debate with herself and reluctantly blocks herself from wedding Hamilton.

★ **Person vs. Society:** People in one's town or culture don't like his way of thinking and insist he conform as he fights the system. First, Hamilton succeeds against restrictive society, in the person of the stodgy Seabury in "Farmer Refuted." Later, Hamilton's Reynolds Pamphlet scandalizes all of New York, to the point where his opponents sing "Never gonna be president now." By breaking society's rules, then publicly confessing and defending himself, Hamilton destroys himself in their eyes. Angelica also struggles with society's expectations when she thinks in "Satisfied": "the gossip in New York City is insidious."

★ **Person vs. Technology:** The protagonist must overcome a machine before it destroys him. Admittedly, not much of this in the story.

GENRE

Genres are categories of the type of writing – drama or fiction is a category, as are types of each of these. The main genres for Hamilton *are historical-fiction musical, but there are certainly moments that fit it into other categories like romance or epic.*

* **Adaptation:** Obviously, the musical reimagines history, with the main characters now of different races, with lots of rap for self-expression. Further, *Hamilton* began as "The Hamilton Mixtape" before Miranda adapted it into a full musical. In this new version, there are many historical changes for the sake of story or simplicity, such as removing many of Hamilton's children and the Schuyler sisters' siblings.

* **Adventure:** Hamilton leaves his island to travel to a far-off land at the show's beginning, and then soon heads for war.

* **Biography:** True narrative of a person's life. Certainly, this is a biography, basically accurate with a few fictional liberties. There are traces of autobiography as Hamilton tells his own story in "The Reynolds Pamphlet."

* **Classic:** Fiction that has become part of an accepted literary canon, widely taught in schools. Fans can be confident this one's heading for schools across America, at least to the theater department.

* **Comedy:** A lighthearted, humorous story characterized by a happy ending for most. There are comedic moments and songs, especially King George's part, but this is, overall, not a comedy, since the hero heads toward tragedy and death, destroying many other lives in the process.

* **Dark comedy/black comedy:** Making fun of something usually considered taboo. This has the effect of making the audience a bit uncomfortable. Hamilton's mocking the king of France's horrific

death by pretending to ask his severed head for advice does this.

★ **Diaries and Journals:** First person writing, usually meant for only private reading, whereas letters are meant to be shared with the receiver. The show presents and quotes from many letters and published essays and articles, but no truly private writings.

★ **Drama:** Fiction that is performed, with actors on stage in front of a live audience. Certainly, the show is this genre.

★ **Epic/saga:** A larger-than-life story, of heroic or legendary figures or the history of a nation. Absolutely this qualifies as the hero defines and creates America.

★ **Epistolary:** A piece of literature told only through letters. The song "Your Obedient Servant" is completely epistolary.

★ **Essay:** A short literary composition that defends a thesis. Seabury reads/sings his in "Farmer Refuted" and Hamilton writes many, especially the Federalist Papers.

★ **Eulogy:** A speech or writing in praise of a person, often deceased. The opening and closing numbers function as these, with the characters considering Hamilton's effect on them and on the world. In the final number, especially, Hamilton's survivors, Eliza, Burr, Jefferson, and Madison, discuss his legacy.

★ **Fan fiction:** Unlicensed fiction about popular characters, usually published free on the internet. History is not copyrighted, but this work – rewriting the characters to be different races than historically true, with a modern rap take on history – feels close.

★ **Fantasy:** Since this fiction has strange or otherworldly settings and invites suspension of reality, the alternate reality modern characters give it a fantasy touch.

★ **Farce:** A ridiculous scene, exaggerated to the point where it's improbable. As Seabury debates and Hamilton mocks him, saying he has mange and that he's completely out of touch, the moment devolves to this.

★ **Fiction:** A story that is made up. A few moments of the show are fictional, especially the dialogue, but the overall plot is basically accurate.

★ **Generational Cycle:** Events of each generation affect the next, who must struggle with the burden. Hamilton and Burr's fathers were both absent, so the heroes try to break the generational cycle and promise Philip and Theodosia in "Dear Theodosia" that they'll stay close. While they keep these promises as well as they can, in history, Hamilton actually died when his youngest child, also named Philip, was only two. Meanwhile, Hamilton feels such sympathy for Maria Reynolds, most likely because she reminds him of his mother: Both of them were trapped in unhappy marriages with spousal abandonment and desperate financial issues. From the moment Young Philip begins rapping, Philip recreates Hamilton's personality and much of his mistakes. He's aware of his own intelligence, and passionately defends what he cares about without considering consequences. He and Hamilton, not learning from each other's mistakes, die the same way.

★ **Gothic:** Ghosts, monsters, and spooky scenes, or madness and trauma. The purple lights of "The Room Where it Happens," as Burr dances and plots, nods to this.

★ **Historical fiction:** Story with fictional characters and events in a historical setting. This is the closest genre to *Hamilton* – retelling history but with dialogue and moments elaborating on history.

★ **History book:** The show quotes from historical documents at times, but many anachronisms, new dialogue, and small changes makes this much more correctly described as historical fiction.

* **Humor:** Silly fiction meant to entertain and sometimes cause intended laughter. There are many humorous moments in the show.
* **Improvisation:** Scenes or moments the actor makes up or adapts on the spot. There are several famous moments of improvisation from the show which became part of the writing later, like the king shouting "Everybody!" at the end of his number or Miranda growling a bit of his courtship song to Eliza.
* **Legend:** Story of a larger-than-life national or folk hero. Partially factual but also imaginative. Definitely qualifies.
* **Linear narrative:** Showing events in order. Most of the musical follows this pattern.
* **Lyrics:** The lines of songs. Basically the entire musical is in lyrics.
* **Melodrama:** Sensational and emotional plot with shallow clichéd characters like "supervillain" and "damsel," all easily identifiable. There are traces of this old-fashioned style as Burr dresses in dark clothes to signify his status as an antagonist and Maria Reynolds wears a blood-red gown and deep red lipstick to emphasize she's the temptress. However, in melodrama, all issues are resolved in a well-defined way with little or no shadows or doubts. The ambiguity of who are the heroes versus the villains makes this far from melodrama.
* **Memoir:** Factual story in which the narrator focuses on significant moments of his/her life and how they transformed him/her. The fact that Burr tells this story and then Eliza finishes it gives the musical a touch of this.
* **Metafiction:** Self-referential fiction that draws attention to itself as a work of art while exposing the "truth" of a story

* **Monomyth:** A hero's journey in which other characters reflect hidden aspects of the hero. For instance, "Together the two eldest sisters formed a complete portrait of Hamilton's ideal woman, each appealing to a different facet of his personality. Eliza reflected Hamilton's earnest sense of purpose, determination, and moral rectitude, while Angelica exhibited his worldly side – the wit, charm, and vivacity that so delighted people" (Chernow 133).

> A Jungian interpretation has Hamilton as hero with all the other characters voicing parts of his personality – Washington represents fatherly advice and experienced wisdom, like Yoda. The loss of Hamilton's mother fills him with survivor guilt and despair, as seen in "Hurricane." Gentle Laurens, who dreams of a world without slavery, is like Hamilton's naiveté – with the same actor playing his son, both characters embody his grand hopes for all the new country can be. Both, of course, soon perish. Mulligan is Hamilton's adventure spirit, and Lafayette, his potential, as both become war heroes and guide Hamilton to do the same. However, in the gloomier Act II, the pair are directly replaced by Hamilton's political rivals, now scheming to bring him down instead of raise him up. In the same way that Frodo's cheerful cousins, Merry and Pippin, give place to the scheming Gollum in *The Lord of the Rings*, Hamilton has entered a darker story and his companions tempt him into despair. Nonetheless, these friends all help teach him about what it means to be a patriot. (Frankel)

* **Musical:** A performance with spoken dialogue, singing, and dancing. *Hamilton* is of course a popular musical. It began off-Broadway then moved to Broadway (a reference to location as well as its big-budget, mainstream status). After a record-setting 16 nominations for the Tony Award – the biggest award for musical theater each year – it won 11.

* **Mystery:** Fiction dealing with the solution of a crime or the unraveling of secrets. There isn't much mystery

here, as Jefferson and his friends investigate the scandal of the Reynolds Pamphlet only to have Hamilton instantly confess.

★ **Mythopoeia:** Fiction in which characters from mythology, folklore and/or history are recast into a re-imagined realm created by the author. Certainly, this recasts the Founding Fathers as semi-modern characters in a world of slang and rap.

★ **Narrative:** A story, a sequence of connected events, whether real or fictional. The full plot arc appears in Hamilton's tale, with a few smaller stories appearing in exposition.

★ **Narrative nonfiction/personal narrative:** Factual information about a significant event presented in a format which tells a story. Historical fiction is a closer term for the musical, but it is clearly adapting the facts of history into a story.

★ **Nautical story:** Most of the drama takes place on a ship. Though Hamilton (and later other characters) sail by ship, none of the scenes take place on board, so it's really not a nautical story. "Hurricane" comes close, but this is an expended metaphor, not what's really happening.

★ **Nonlinear narrative:** Showing events out of order. The frame story, in which Burr gives away the ending, and Angelica's flashback of "Satisfied" depart from the story's traditional pattern.

★ **Opera, operetta:** An opera is a drama completely sung with no spoken words. An operetta only has a few. A musical is a mix of spoken and sung. *Hamilton* was created as a musical, but the fact that very little is spoken without being rapped pushes it close to operetta.

★ **Paranoid drama:** The main character devolves into suspicion, thinking everyone's out to get him. Near the end of the show, Hamilton thinks the whole world has turned on him, to the point where he decides the Reynolds Pamphlet is a good idea. Eliza protests in "Burn": "Your sentences border on senseless/And you are paranoid in every paragraph."

★ **Parody:** A silly imitation for purpose of ridicule. Hamilton parodies Jefferson's plan by pretending to honor their treaty by asking King Louis's dead head in a basket what they should do, and giving its mocking answer.

★ **Philosophical story:** One that spends most of the work considering the meaning of a soul, the purpose of life, etc. This musical asks philosophical questions about moral choices and the best path for the country, but focuses more on the characters and plot.

★ **Picaresque:** The adventures of a roguish hero of low social class who lives by his or her wits in a corrupt society. Hamilton is more classic hero than the thief or swindler usually seen here. The scenes with Maria Reynolds likely come the closest as he acts immorally and tries to get ahead, as do Mr. and Mrs. Reynolds.

★ **Play:** A drama performed onstage. While this general term, like show, can often be used to cover several genres, *Hamilton* is more correctly a musical.

★ **Poetry:** Lines that have rhyme, rhythm, or other patterns. Basically all the lines of the show are written this way, though since they're song lines calling them "lyrics" is more accurate.

★ **Postmodern:** The postmodern genre deconstructs the nature of writing through metafiction, retellings, satire, and more. This story certainly questions the Founding Fathers' role as white slaveowners, as well as containing many metafictional moments.

★ **Prose:** Ordinary, nonpoetic sentences. A few significant moments of the show are prose, as when Burr straightforwardly summarizes how many of the Federalist Papers Hamilton wrote.

★ **Realistic:** A story with no fantasy, one that takes place in the real world. *Hamilton* is historical, but with enough anachronism of the two time periods combined that it doesn't really fit this.

★ **Romance:** A story focusing on relationships. The Eliza-Hamilton-Angelica love triangle is central to the story, dominating enough of it that the musical might certainly called a historical romance. There are also a few romance novels about Hamilton and Eliza.

★ **Satire:** A literary style used to ridicule. This might be silly like *The Simpsons* or serious like *The Hunger Games*. Hamilton mocks Seabury and Jefferson while debating with them and Adams in his open letter. Further the show satirizes King George by making him look like an immature bully.

★ **Speech:** Public address. The vital quality of a speech is that there's an audience listening and being swayed. "Farmer Refuted" has Hamilton and Seabury hilariously making speeches over each other, with Hamilton mimicking the rhymes and tunes of his opponent while also criticizing his delivery and content.

★ **Suspense/Thriller:** The main character is in terrible danger and tries to escape it. While the battle scenes are brief, the duels draw out suspense as much as possible to increase the drama.

★ **Tall tale:** Humorous story with blatant exaggerations. Most of the show is historically true, but Martha Washington naming her tomcat after Hamilton may be one of these.

★ **Tragedy:** Drama based on human suffering, generally ending with catharsis or revelation. The plot arc of Act II is arguably a tragedy, since Hamilton dies young, unable to accomplish much of what he had to offer. Further, he brings it on himself with his arrogance and outspoken insults. This is a tragic flaw in the protagonist, common to tragic stories. Chernow explains further:

> I think that he felt that fate had handed him an opportunity to reinvent himself and to start life over. But I don't think that he ever fully left the world of his childhood behind him. He was poor, he was illegitimate, he was ashamed of all of those things. And even though he tried so hard to escape, on some level he was always trapped back in the darkness of that boyhood. (*Alexander Hamilton: American Experience*)

★ **Tragicomedy:** tragedy that ends happily. The reverse would be more true for this show.

★ **Urban fiction:** This means a story that takes place in a city, and *Hamilton* is certainly a New York epic. Admittedly, urban fiction is often contemporary, though this isn't required.

PLOT

Dramatic structure (also called Freytag's pyramid) contains the basic steps of a story:

★ **Exposition/backstory:** Background information in the story. It's the set-up, the character's biography before the adventure starts. The opening number provides much of this, as does Burr as he sets the scene and summarizes what's happened over and over through the story.

★ **Initiating incident:** Something that propels the character into his adventure. Hamilton's hurricane, which encouraged the islanders to chip in for a scholarship, and his meeting the Revolutionaries both qualify.

★ **Rising action:** Events build through the story. Hamilton fights in the war and works in politics, all the while having moments that push him towards his final conflict.

★ **Climax:** The turning point, which changes the protagonist's fate, in which he risks all and wins or loses the story. While Hamilton has several moments like this, his final duel with Burr is the story's main climax.

★ **Falling action:** This is much shorter than the rising action, and wraps up the characters' fates. On the show, this is very short, but Burr ruminates on how destructive his choices have been.

★ **Dénouement/resolution:** The conclusion of the story, mostly provided in the show by Eliza who tells of Hamilton's legacy and its importance.

Other Terms

★ **Catharsis:** (cleansing) The releasing of strong emotions, especially pity and fear. By watching the main character in a tragedy, the audience can find resolution within themselves. Hamilton's grief at his son's death and monologue during his own have this effect.

★ **Cliffhanger:** The audience is left in suspense when the character remains in mortal danger, generally at the end of a chapter, episode, etc. Act I resolves much of the conflict, but there's a cliffhanger over how Hamilton will balance ambition and family ties.

★ **Deus ex machina** (God in a box): The conflict is wrapped up by someone, often a god in Greek drama, arriving to tell the character what he's done and how it has caused his own downfall. Or the god may abruptly hand out rewards and punishments Angelica's diatribe against Hamilton after the Reynolds Pamphlet (trimmed down from the cut song "Congratulations") fulfils this trope.

★ **Epilogue:** An afterward to the story, summing up what happened, often much later. "Who Lives Who Dies, Who Tells Your Story" is this.

★ **Eucatastrophe:** A term from J. R. R. Tolkien for a sudden salvation and *lack* of catastrophe. Yorktown meets this trope as the Colonists expect doom but abruptly triumph.

★ **Flashback:** A glimpse of the past. The clever flashback in the musical, complete with the turntable and characters rewinding like a tape, covers the sisters meeting Alexander from a new angle. The distorted sound design plays along with the turntable effect, as if Angelica herself is skipping or scratching as she reaches into her memories. This skipping insistently repeats Angelica's act of remembrance ("I remember that night I just might, I remember that night, I remember that"), which suggests that she's been compulsively replaying that night in her memories, doubting and regretting her decision all the way up to Eliza's wedding. This rewind alters the meaning of what's come before. "Helpless" is a sweet straightforward love song of Eliza's love for him and their courtship. "Satisfied," just after, shows the conversation from Angelica's point of view and it suddenly becomes a tragic song of self-sacrifice.

★ **Flashforward:** Showing what will happen in the future. "Who Lives, Who Dies, Who Tells Your Story" arguably does this, covering the next fifty years of Eliza's life.

★ **Framing device:** The same element – such as a setting, event, or piece of music – is used at both the beginning and the end of the work. This allows a second story, often one explaining what will happen in the other, or why it's being told. The first and last numbers of *Hamilton* use this technique, creating a story within a story.

★ **In medias res:** Opening a story in the middle of the action. With its heavy prologue, *Hamilton* does not do this.

★ **Obstacles:** Problems, including characters, that stop or delay the hero's success.

★ **Pace:** How fast or slow the story feels. Short sentences, fast music, shocking events, and action scenes can speed it up.

★ **Plot twist:** A new element or surprise that the audience wasn't expecting.

★ **Poetic justice:** Like with karma, good characters are rewarded and bad characters are punished. Not required in stories, and rather ambiguous in *Hamilton* as none of the characters are completely good or bad and the antagonists Jefferson and Madison become presidents, while sympathetic Hamilton and Burr fall into tragedy.

★ **Prologue:** Setting up the story beforehand with a summary or event outside the main plot. "Alexander Hamilton," which sets up and summarizes, is this.

★ **Reveal:** In this plot device, a large secret is brought to light. The Reynolds Pamphlet qualifies, though the events were known to the audience, if not all the characters.

★ **Scene changes:** A change of setting, as characters move from being in the war to being in Eliza's house. Sometimes these are marked by changes in lighting or furniture, sometimes not.

★ **Scenes:** The story itself with moment-by-moment action and dialogue. Most of the musical is in scenes, with Burr setting the stage in brief moments of exposition.

★ **Self-fulfilling prophecy:** The hero makes his destiny happen, often while trying to avoid it. If Hamilton's destiny is laid out in the prologue as getting shot by Burr, he certainly brings it about himself, with several crucial moments in "The Election of 1800" and "Your Obedient Servant." Setting up the story in this way makes it a narrative of Hamilton trying to avoid his inevitable fate, though he's all the more doomed because it's historical fact.

★ **Subplot:** A smaller plot with little or no effect on the larger one. If the plot follows Hamilton's rise from orphan immigrant to Founding Father, then his love triangle and Burr's ambition are subplots. Several subplots, like Burr's wife's death and Ben Franklin's adventures in France were cut for being too far off topic.

★ **Surprise:** The audience has no idea what's coming and is shocked when it comes out of nowhere. Philip's death shocked many audience members who didn't know the history.

★ **Suspense:** The opposite of surprise. The audience knows what's going to happen and tension comes from how slowly it arrives – i.e., the events of the story are all leading towards Hamilton and Burr's final duel, as set up in the prologue.

POINT OF VIEW

Who's telling the story – a character, a narrator, etc.

★ **Author:** The author wrote the words, but the person telling the story may be a persona, a narrator with a different personality than the author's.

★ **First person:** Use of "I" or "we." Burr tells his own story using this form, and sometimes other characters like Hamilton do the same.

★ **Multiple narrators:** The opening and closing numbers offer this. Further, a cut version of the final duel had Hamilton and Burr each reprising "Ten Duel Commandments" and explaining their thoughts during the scene.

★ **Narrator:** The one telling the story. This is Burr, though ironically, Miranda, playing Hamilton, wrote the musical.

★ **Second person:** Use of you, or speaking directly to the audience. Burr tells the audience of Hamilton in the opening number, "See if you can spot him."

* **Stream of consciousness:** Babbling one's thoughts without putting them in grammatically correct sentences, in a style that replicates unfiltered feelings. Hamilton's death scene is in this style.
* **Third person limited:** Telling the story using "he" and "they." Limited means the narrator is trapped in one person's head. Burr's lines about "How does an orphan…" suggest this perspective, since he's confused about Hamilton's perspective.
* **Third person omniscient:** Also "he" and "they," but this time, the narrator can leap into anyone's head. "The Room Where It Happens," suggests narrator Burr knows what everyone's thinking.
* **Unreliable narrator:** A narrator whom the audience can't completely believe. Most of the situations in the show appear to have taken place about the way presented. However, Burr emphasizes that he can't narrate the events between Maria and Hamilton, since no one witnessed it, making many other events a bit murkier. Further, Burr, the narrator, rails and insults each time, emphasizing his hatred of Hamilton, which certainly color the story.

SYMBOLISM

*A **symbol** is anything that stands for something else. **Conventional symbols**, given meaning by society, include a white flag for surrender or stars and stripes for the United States. **Natural symbols** are objects from nature that represent ideas commonly associated with them (dawn after the battle of Yorktown symbolizes a new beginning, while a hurricane symbolizes destruction and lack of control). Meanwhile, **literary symbols** are often specific to the story and how they're used, like the many uses of "My shot." In the show, clothes, lighting, song titles and other nonspoken aspects can all contribute to these:*

★ Most of the set is wooden scaffolding of a sort. The stage back includes a partially built brick wall, and it grows by more feet during intermission, echoing the building of the country. Set designer David Korins explains:

> We came up with a couple of different ideas. One was that the surround was a theatrical metaphor of sorts for what was actually happening at the time in the country. It is architecturally like a tapestry of early American architecture. At that time, the carpenters were actually ship builders. The building methodologies they employed were ones of boat builders. We carried that into our set, you see all of the seams and all the joints that made up all the boards and beams, all come from ship building techniques. There's a lot of rope, block and tackle, pulleys and other nautical references... We're not building the inside dome of the Capitol. We're not building the Washington Monument. What we're doing is we are building the kind of structure that is the scaffolding and the wrapping that we then will build all these things from. (Eddy)

★ The opening number "Alexander Hamilton" shows everyone in white, from main characters to Hamilton himself. The ghostliness of the cast echoes the tragedy and loss in the historical Hamilton's life. They've stepped from the pages of a book or out of the mists of history, then later focus into color. Only Burr, the central narrator, has a red coat, suggesting power, pride, and battle as well as a vital role here – more vital in some ways than Hamilton's.

★ Eliza brings Hamilton a brown coat, suggesting a new role for him, as well as her own role as his seamstress and homemaker. He hands the white coat to Burr, emphasizing his antagonist's role as helper in this biography. Angelica gives him books, nodding to their intellectual flirtations, and Laurens gives him a travel bag that suggests their friendship and his soldier's kit – he and Laurens will be aides-de-camp together.

* The stairs descend, suggesting a set being fashioned around him.
* When Burr confesses, "I'm the damn fool that shot him," he stands center stage, full in the spotlight, but stumbles at Hamilton comes up from behind him and takes his place – reflecting their roles in the story.
* Hamilton wears brown (suggesting his humble origins and obscurity) when he and Burr meet, with Burr still in the royal red of wealth and privilege, also hinting at his devil role.
* In "My Shot," the other tavern patrons sing and dance with Hamilton, and the scene opens to the streets of New York and lit up scaffolding, with even more eager listeners, emphasizing how the word is spreading wider and wider. The turntable in the floor spins, suggesting Hamilton's message is spreading through the colonies and that the world is spinning into something new.
* Hamilton dances with hand over his heart, with the multicultural crowd no longer washed-out like ghosts but lit in vibrant gold. The crowd mirrors his dance, as an extension of his passion. Hamilton soon switches from singing with the crowd to rapping on his own, emphasizing how he'll stand out as an individual.
* Exploring the city, the Schuyler sisters wear three colors: Eliza's soft green shows her as a nurturer, carer for things that grow, like Hamilton and the new country. Peggy's yellow is youthful and innocent. Eliza's pink-peach is hotter and more sensual.
* The king represents the old world, since he's the only white main character. He even dresses traditionally, in the real royal robes, and stands statically, criticizing the action instead of participating. Unlike the Founding Fathers, he always sings alone. His are the most "traditional musical theatre" numbers. With this, he suggests all the old rules of monarchy and musical

theater together. His songs are even styled after the British Invasion, in a subtle pun.

★ In contrast with the king's red-purple light, Washington contrasts him completely, marching powerfully with blue light and blue uniform coat. His color scheme suggests the British naval invasion he enters on and Washington's despair as they struggle to win against near-impossible odds.

★ Washington gives Hamilton a pen, emphasizing that he will be Washington's voice, not his soldier. Of course, his role as wordsmith will continue through the show. As Hamilton takes the position, the light turns a more hopeful purple as Hamilton, Washington's capable new sidekick, raps about all he can organize.

★ In "Helpless," the dancers whirl around Eliza on the turntable, lit in pink. It's a romantic scene, emphasized by the color and also her spinning world.

★ In "Ten Duel Commandments," the turntable echoes events spiraling out of control again, and the rings of lights suggest a disturbing bullseye.

★ When Hamilton finally agrees to go home, Eliza is only a step away, symbolizing how the only thing parting him and his wife is himself.

★ By "Guns and Ships," Lafayette, who couldn't pronounce "anarchy" earlier, now raps faster than anyone in the show. His actor, Daveed Diggs, notes, "Lafayette has to figure it out. Lafayette is rapping in a real like simple early eighties style rap cadence at first and then by the end he's doing his crazy double and triple time things" (*Hamilton's America*). As Miranda puts it, "He goes from being one of Hamilton's friends to a rap god/military superhero" once he's put in command (*Hamilton: The Revolution* 119).

★ Eliza helps Hamilton with his coat when he departs on this new adventure, and Washington gives him a sword, paralleling the previous scene with the pen but promoting him at last.

★ "A world turned upside down" has multiple meanings – they are in a revolution and the chaos of war, but also they are trying to flip the world and govern themselves.

★ As Yorktown is won, each soldier plants himself on a table or stool with Hamilton on his soapbox – this is like the tavern celebrations but much stiller, bookending their path to freedom. The light turns golden brown like dawn, but it's striped with shadows like gravestones or bars – there's still darkness and uncertainty.

★ After this, Hamilton and Burr each sing to their children. In shirtsleeves, they have a moment of similarity as well as vulnerability. They sing in chairs side by side in identical squares of light that suggest nursery windows but also the responsibility and permanence of domesticity.

> The lights transform to a circle of Hamilton's courtroom, though once more there's the suggestion of a target, blending motifs from war to court. Burr introduces the lyrics and music of Hamilton's writing "like you're running out of time" in a bouncy, Caribbean-beat samba-reggae number. The staging is a whirlwind of spinning as Hamilton rushes from activity to activity, lecturing fellow politicians in their chairs, writing at his desk, defending a client in court. A green light for Hamilton writing and doing legal business appears as a new motif. As it happens, the real Hamilton's study was also money green. He wrote constantly, carrying a portable writing desk everywhere, even on horseback (*Hamilton's America*). (Frankel)

★ In "Non-Stop," Angelica sails off and Eliza replaces her, then they tug at him as they sing their lyric on either side of him. In this moment, they particularly represent two sides of him – satisfaction versus ambition. Hamilton climbs the steps to join Washington, suggesting a promotion.

> With Madison fully clothed in grey and Jefferson in plum, the characters have graduated from the ensemble's white suits to be fully actualized. They won't keep switching roles but will stay politicians for all of Act II. The coat changes suggest growth as well as the passage of time – new outfits mean new roles and responsibilities. Washington wears stately black with Hamilton now fully in green. Hamilton adds glasses eventually, showing his age by the end. Green nods to his treasury role and financial success. The green also sets him in opposition to Jefferson, whose loose hair, long purple coat, and velvet waistcoat all stress his love of luxury. (Frankel)

★ "Washington on your Side" begins lit in red, then as the men plan, the lights flash and cries of "oh" resemble cannon fire. Political warfare is symbolically a real war as the ensemble line up behind Jefferson, Madison, and Burr like an army.

★ Washington and Hamilton say their goodbyes both wearing black with shirtsleeves showing – they're looking vulnerable and casual as well as identical – working as a team as they did in the war.

★ In "The Room Where it Happens," Burr's misery at being excluded is clear. Madison, Hamilton, and Jefferson close themselves in a light square, shutting Burr out in the dark. The ensemble dance in more squares around him, once more shutting him out.

★ Hamilton sings "Hurricane" about how he "wrote my way out" of poverty. "The ensemble are frozen around him, crumpled, then struggling against the blue-purple storm, whisking his desk and chair away like a force of wind. The bursts of chords resemble a pounding gale. The turntable spins, leaving him in the hurricane's glowing eye. Elements of his life and memories all are whirling around him, out of control"

(Frankel). "The last thing that we added was the double turntable," explains set designer David Korins.

> I just couldn't get out of my head the swirling, cyclical motion of the storytelling. It starts with Alexander Hamilton living on the island of Nevis and it gets swept over by a swirling hurricane. That idea, the cyclical swirling continues throughout the themes of the show: including in political struggles, in his sex scandal, the cyclical nature of his relationship with Burr, and on and on. (Eddy)

★ "In fact, while Burr is locked in with squares, Hamilton's world is constantly turning, like his quick mind and revolving circumstances – surprising luck and surprising disaster. His own cleverness and ego cause one then the other" (Frankel).

★ In "The Reynolds Pamphlet," papers go around the stage, but lights flash and speakers boom, like thunder and lightning. This explosion suggests Hamilton has blown up his own world.

★ Eliza's refrain and the song title "Burn" is an insult, suggesting her anger in modern terms, but she also condemns him to hell with her final line "I hope that you burn." Meanwhile, she literally burns the letters onstage, ending a stage of their relationship.

★ It's the woman who plays the Bullet who tells Philip where to find Eaker for the duel, setting up his and his father's deaths.

> In this duel, there's no target shape, just white spotlights, but the ensemble in their white suggest the ghosts Philip will join. He's wounded and carried off. His mother arrives, already in black just as Hamilton sings "Stay Alive" to his son, taking the lyrics for himself as he finds himself cast as helpless family, no longer the daredevil hero. The light is the blue of memory and despair as Eliza recalls her son's piano lessons, with the count of ten reimagined from the duel into death. In his own muted grey, Philip shares the touching song with his parents and dies. In black as well, Angelica, a

> close outsider like Burr, takes over the narration for a moment. "There are moments that the words don't reach/There is suffering too terrible to name," she sings as the parents stand stunned and silent in black, barely lit in dark purple. (Frankel)

★ The song of "Hamilton on your Side," as Madison suggests Jefferson get Hamilton's endorsement, shows that Hamilton has stepped into Washington's shoes as older statesman.

★ The actress playing the Bullet continues driving the characters toward tragedy: "The Bullet actually pulls Burr's desk onto the stage and hands him his quill so that he can begin his fateful letters, edging his toward the battlefield. Every action she takes ensures that Hamilton meets her one last time" (Corde).

★ As the crowd ask Hamilton to choose between Jefferson and Burr, red and white stripes spread, and a circle alternating red and white, suggesting not just patriotism but partisanship. Of course, the suggestion of a target is also important here, as Hamilton dooms himself with the endorsement.

> When Hamilton bids Eliza goodbye, she's in a blue dressing gown, suggesting the intimate privacy of their home. Blue is a maternal color, seen in the cloak of the Virgin Mary. Shortly after, she will cast off the robe to return to the white gown. Since her black dress is also an overgown on the white gown, Eliza is the one to now quick-switch roles from happy wife (green) to the betrayed bride of "Burn" (white), to bereft mother (black) to loving but saddened wife (blue) to angelic spirit and eternal biographer (white). It's Hamilton who's stopped changing. (Frankel)

★ Hamilton and Burr duel, dressing identically at the end in black greatcoats, suggesting they've been coming closer and closer as they head towards their inevitable ending. The red and golden target flashes on the floor, suggesting the drama and violence of the moment.

★ In his final monologue, Hamilton creates metaphors about legacy: "It's planting seeds in a garden you never get to see; I wrote some notes at the beginning of a song someone will sing for me." Both of these symbolize what he's built.

> [The Bullet] appears for a final time as the actual bullet, slowly approaching Hamilton throughout the entirety of his final monologue and coming dangerously close to him as he moves, scatter-brained, across the stage. Halfway through, he steps right in her path, turns back and stumbles out of the way, and as he frantically repeats, "Rise up, rise up, rise up," she lunges for him, only to be pulled back by another ensemble member as Eliza steps in her path. Once Hamilton has been shot, she joins the ensemble once again, satisfied that the path she's been on since the beginning has come to an end. (Corde)

★ "His final line, 'Raise a glass to freedom!' salutes his dead friends in their tavern, the journey he embarked on in 'My Shot' and the new country he helped build. It also visually resembles raising his pistol to the sky" (Frankel).

★ In her white gown and pink light, blending the romance of their courtship with the ghostly timeless purity of the prologue, Eliza tells about Hamilton's legacy, now taking the narrator role.

> Onstage, Eliza sings about seeing him again until Hamilton arrives to take her hand and escort her for a moment, whirling in their ever-present cycle. She gasps in her pink light, suggesting she has found her Hamilton again even as she dies. Thus their story ends. An alternate theory is that Eliza's gasp comes as the fourth wall falls and she beholds the audience, discovering that the story she's telling really does matter to history – she has succeeded in her final mission. In this case, the figure escorting her might not be Hamilton but the

show's creator Lin-Manuel Miranda, revealing to her the audience she's earned. (Frankel)

WORKS CITED

Alexander Hamilton: American Experience, written by Ronald Blumer, produced and directed by Muffie Meyer, PBS, 2007.
    http://www.pbs.org/wgbh/amex/hamilton/filmmore/pt.html.

Berman, Eliza. "Hamilton Nation." *Time,* vol. 188, no. 14, 2016, pp. 50. *MasterFILE Premier.*

Binelli, Mark. "Hamilton Mania." *Rolling Stone,* vol. 1263, 2016, pp. 36. MasterFILE Premier.

Bradner, Eric. "Pence: 'I wasn't offended' by Message of *Hamilton* Cast." *CNN Politics,* 20 Nov. 2016.
    http://www.cnn.com/2016/11/20/politics/mike-pence-hamilton-message-trump.

Chernow, Ron. *Alexander Hamilton.* Penguin Books, 2005.

Corde, Phoebe. "The Piece of Foreshadowing in *Hamilton* That Everyone Misses." *Odyssey,* 19 Sept 2016.
    https://www.theodysseyonline.com/piece-foreshadowing-hamilton-misses.

DiGiacomo, Frank. "*Hamilton's* Lin-Manuel Miranda on Finding Originality, Racial Politics (and Why Trump Should See His Show)." *Hollywood Reporter,* 12 Aug. 2015.
    http://www.hollywoodreporter.com/features/hamiltons-lin-manuel-miranda-finding-814657.

Dreamcatcher. "All Deleted Songs from *Hamilton.*" 6 Dec. 2016.
    https://www.youtube.com/watch?v=EZkANYGycNU.

"The Duel," *The American Experience, PBS.org,* 2000.
    http://www.pbs.org/wgbh/amex/duel/filmmore/reference/interview/freeman08.html

Eddy, Michael S. "A Scaffold to Build a Nation On." *Stage Directions,* vol. 28, no.10, 2015, pp. 10. *MasterFILE Premier.*

Evans, Suzy. "The Room Where It Happens." *American Theatre,* vol. 32, no. 7, 2015, pp. 26. *MasterFILE Premier.*

Frankel, Valerie Estelle. *Who Tells Your Story: History, Pop Culture, and Hidden Meanings in the Musical Phenomenon Hamilton.* LitCrit Press, 2016.

"Going H.A.M.: A Track-By-Track Review of the *Hamilton* Soundtrack." *Vibe*, Oct. 2015. http://www.vibe.com/2015/10/hamilton-soundtrack-review.

"Hamilton: A Founding Father Takes to the Stage." *YouTube*, uploaded by *CBS Sunday Morning*, 8 Mar. 2015. https://www.youtube.com/watch?v=0wboCdgzLHg.

James, Kendra. "Race, Immigration, and Hamilton: The Relevance of Lin-Manuel Miranda's New Musical." *The Toast*, 1 Oct 2015. http://the-toast.net/2015/10/01/race-immigration-and-hamilton.

Jones, Nate. "Nerding Out With Hamilton Musical Director, Alex Lacamoire," *Vulture*, 13 Jan 2016. http://www.vulture.com/2016/01/hamilton-alex-lacamoire-interview.html

Maggregor, Jeff. "The Maestro." *Smithsonian*, vol. 46, no. 8, 2015, pp. 52. *MasterFILE Premier.*

McWhorter, John. "Will *Hamilton* Save The Musical? Don't Wait For It." *American Theatre*, vol. 33, no. 3, 2016, pp. 48. *MasterFILE Premier.*

Mead, Rebecca. "All About the Hamiltons." *The New Yorker*, 9 Feb. 2015. http://www.newyorker.com/magazine/2015/02/09/hamiltons

Miranda, Lin-Manuel and Jeremy McCarter. *Hamilton: The Revolution.* Hachette Book Group, 2016.

Obama, Barak. "Remarks Prior to a Musical Performance by Members of the Cast of "Hamilton." *Daily Compilation of Presidential Documents*, 2016, pp. 1. MasterFILE Premier.

Smith, Kyle. "Dueling Misfits." *New Criterion* vol. 34, no. 2, 2015, pp. 39. *MasterFILE Premier.*

Solomon, Alisa. "A Modern Major Musical." *Nation*, vol. 301, no. 11/12, 2015, pp. 27. *MasterFILE Premier.*

Tommasini, Anthony and Jon Caramanica "Exploring

'Hamilton' and Hip-Hop Steeped in Heritage." *The New York Times*, 30 Aug. 2015. http://www.nytimes.com/2015/08/30/theater/explorin g-hamilton-and-hip-hop-steeped-in-heritage.html.

Viertel, Jack. *The Secret Life of the American Musical.* Sarah Crichton Books, 2016.

ABOUT THE AUTHOR

Valerie Estelle Frankel is the author of many books on pop culture, including *Doctor Who – The What, Where, and How, Sherlock: Every Canon Reference You May Have Missed in BBC's Series 1-3, History, Homages and the Highlands: An Outlander Guide,* and *How Game of Thrones Will End.* Many of her books focus on women's roles in fiction, from her heroine's journey guides *From Girl to Goddess* and *Buffy and the Heroine's Journey* to books like *Women in Game of Thrones* and *The Many Faces of Katniss Everdeen.* Once a lecturer at San Jose State University, she's a frequent speaker at conferences. Come explore her research at www.vefrankel.com.

Made in the USA
Columbia, SC
11 January 2019